# Stomper

## Listening in the Silence

---

## Author - Craig Hedges

## Illustrator - Clint Hedges

Craig Hedges

# DEDICATION

This book is dedicated to my wife and kids. Without you I would have never attempted this project. In the days I doubted I could, your faith in me was unfailing. Thank you for enduring the roller coaster that is Craig Hedges. I love you more!

# CONTENTS

# ACKNOWLEDGMENTS

To my kids. Hannah, Isaac, Ian and Eli, you are my source of inspiration. The conversations we have and the plans we are making toward a better tomorrow are what gets me out of bed every day. You are the best, and I love you!

To Keith Russell. Your friendship is so greatly appreciated. Thank you for your edits and encouragement through this process!

And to you, yes you reading this right now. Thank you so much for your support in my telling of our stories through our life. I pray the words of this book provide you with inspiration and a bit of hope that life is worth every trial. It's a great life you have, if you learn the lessons and make it a little better tomorrow.

## CHAPTER 1 - ADOPTION

As a happy father of four and husband of one, I want to share my life changing story with you. I am sure you can recall moments in your life that were pivotal to bring you to where you are right now. Some may have been inopportune or even inconvenient, but if you look back with an open mind you will see that without that moment you wouldn't be who you are today. This is the true story of how one phone call changed my family forever.

Ring......

The call could not have come at a worse time. I had moved my family to Maine, and had only been there about five months. During this time we had already moved once, and were planning our second move. My wife, Tammy, was from Maine, and I was just an ole' Kentucky boy. Tammy had lived in the south since about the age of thirteen, and upon our return she scarcely remembered this place. So much had changed. It wasn't the landscape, but the role she found herself in now. As a little girl, someone else was responsible for keeping the frigid temperatures at bay. Now it was on our shoulders to provide a house warm enough that our children would not see their breath on every exhale. We had packed our belongings and driven eighteen-hundred miles with our four kids so that I could accept a job at a large bank. We had been living within two miles of my family for the last fifteen years. This opportunity would give us the chance to to be near Tammy's family for a change. Until that point we only visited for a week or so every few years.

We encountered our first nor'easter in mid-January, two days after we moved into our rental house. A nor'easter is a storm whose strongest winds blow from northeast to southwest, and those winds are usually accompanies by a few feet of snow. Our first nor'easter dropped twenty-six inches of snow on us. Was this really happening? We could not even see the front door! Neither the kids nor I had ever seen anything like this. As for Tammy it had been a couple of decades. The excitement on the faces of the kids was that of a second Christmas, but without the tireless decorations. I was undeterred.

After digging around the porch for my snow shovel, I bulldozed a path down the stairs to the outside entrance of our detached garage. When I raised the main garage door, the snow drift was an inch from the shoulder height on my 5' 9.5" frame! From the upper level of the house I hears a muffled yell from one of my kids. Through the skin shredding winds, I cupped my hands to my mouth and asked for a repeat. Tammy slid the window open to magnify the voice, but now it had multiplied.

"Jump!" rang the voices of my family in unison.

Apparently, there is a look that all men give right before they do something rather irrational. It must have beamed from my face, for without a word from me I heard my oldest son, Isaac, laugh through the words, "He's gonna do it!"

Backing into the garage and out of sight of my audience, I took two deep breaths. I ran as hard as I could and jumped full steam into the snow drift, spinning my body so that my back could absorb the impact from what I thought would be snow compacting below me as I landed. That did not happen. Instead, I did not stop falling until I hit concrete. You see, Kentucky snow always has a moisture factor added in. But here in Maine, a Kentucky boy's arctic tundra, the temperatures are sub-zero. Those little, melted ice crystals that I imagined would break my fall were an illusion.

Unexpectedly, three feet of freshly fallen powder moved in concert out of my way to ensure my first (and last) snow jump was an overwhelming failure.

Hitting the concrete and knocking the wind from my flailing body wasn't enough, for the snow then proceeded to fill the void my large frame had left just a few feet from where I had soared haphazardly into the white sea. I was now laying on my back like a corpse, sure that this was a front row seat to my own burial. The abrupt landing cause me to inhale violently. My lungs not only filled with arctic air, but that was followed by shards of ice crystals determined to seal my fate. I freaked.

I came up swinging. I doubtless had crazy in my eyes as I swung my arms ferociously to alert my own brain that I was free. Huge gulps of air and snow were swallowed and released as I tried to gain my bearings. I'm sure it must have been quite the site to my audience. Above me, through the open window, came a roar nothing short of a grossly, overly exaggerated, snort-filled celebration at what my family had just witnessed. This was Maine, and new adventures awaited. A new way of life was staring us in the face, and this was to be the first of many tests that would remind us that the world as we knew it was expanding.

We were only in our first house for three weeks. To say our landlady was incompetent would be an understatement. She cut off our propane heat and expected us to buy space heaters (which we were not comfortable with) to heat the house through the frigid winter. In our signed lease, it stated she was to allow us the use of the remaining propane left in the tank, and we could refill it once that ran out. Needless to say, we brought to her our grievances along with the fact that she had violated her own lease agreement. According to Maine's laws we were free to go. She did not even put up a fight. Not a tear was shed by my family and we could not leave fast enough.

After our first week of living in that house, Tammy had already started looking for an alternate living space. She found a nineteenth century home about a mile away. It was beautiful on the outside with its old school wood siding and beautiful trim around the windows. Five concrete steps led to a small landing by the front door. Opening the solid wood door, you were greeted by original wood flooring. On the left, steep steps led you up to three bedrooms and a full bath. To the right of the front door was the living room, which boasted original crown molding on both the baseboard and the tall, ten-foot ceilings. There was a narrow hall between the steps and the living room leading to the kitchen on the left. The dining room set off to the right of the kitchen and had a doorway connecting the living room.

If you were to set on the couch and look straight through the dining room, you would spot the bonus room which we used as our music room, complete with a drum set we purchased and a keyboard which had been given to us. The music room doubled as a storage room for my ever increasing book collection, along with crafting supplies used by the whole family. From the front entryway, you could look down the narrow hallway into the kitchen and spot the door which led to a second bath, and to our master bedroom.

We heard the same thing over and over from visitors, "Those tall ceilings are going to make it hard to heat this house."

We loved that house, but everyone was right. It was difficult to heat in large part because the windows were old, which caused a draft to run through the house. We hung plastic up around the windows to keep the flow at bay, but it became so drafty that we brought the kids' mattresses downstairs so they could sleep on the living room floor. This was a great way to keep the upstairs heating costs down, and this is how we survived our first winter in Maine. With spring came much greater promise.

The natural foliage in Maine will rival any I've seen in the United States. The entire state takes pride in the fact that their state is so underdeveloped. It is a remote paradise for anyone interested in the great outdoors, wildlife, or for those who may want to reminisce about the simpler times of yesteryear.

We were very optimistic about where we were until the landlords introduced themselves. They were snowbirds, fresh from their home in Florida. They brought back with them devastating news.

"We have to raise your rent by $200 starting next month," they declared.

"What! Why?" I thought.

They explained that winter had been difficult on them financially, and their properties had suffered the brunt. They were raising everyone's rent to offset damages caused by the nor'easters. It was now May, and June would be our last month with the current, lower rate. It was time to find yet again, another house.

The truth is, we knew we were where God wanted us to be. This was the one thing that kept us going in those difficult times. As a family of faith, we had felt the nudge of God to move to Maine and begin a new life in a fresh place. Though the circumstances were far from optimal, we knew we were in the right area. So the search began again. It was time to find yet another house.

Tammy had been scouring the newspapers and internet listings. Her family drove her down a long stretch of road shortly after, and a "FOR RENT" sign caught her eye. She called the listed number and set up a time to see the house. It was a massive farmhouse sitting on the front end of a 250 acre farm. It was love at first site, but there was a catch.

The house had been split into three apartment homes. The full length of the lower level with a 3-car attached garage was one apartment, the living space above the garage was the second apartment, and the full length of the upper level was the third apartment, our living space. We had access to the attic, which was a great place to send our herd of buffalo (our three boys) to play without worrying about the family below us accidentally having a chandelier fall from the rattling stampede above. In addition to the house, we were also granted access to all 250 acres of the farm.

The paperwork was signed, and plans to move yet again were already underway. We were committed to the house, and the kids were informed that they would be changing school districts. Tammy and I were not too excited about the kids changing schools, but once they saw the house we knew they would be ok. There was nothing to do but wait for it to be cleaned from the last tenants.

My sister-in-law, Nadine, had been searching for a new puppy ever since her daughter's boxer passed away following surgery to repair a heart defect. She found a lady who bred them, and white puppies are all she had. Their tails had been bobbed and the first line of shots given. When Nadine went to pick out the one she wanted, she fell in love with a special puppy. His disposition was so sweet and loving, but instead of taking him home, she chose a different one. The sweet little puppy was deaf. Nadine knew that in order to give this pup the life it deserved, it needed someone who understood it better than she.

I have a cousin who is deaf. His name is Doug. I did not get to see Doug much when we were kids because he was in school throughout the week and lived over an hour away. My time with him was spent during the summers. One summer when I was eleven, Doug and his sister, Melody, had taken my brother and I to their pond to play with his new remote controlled boat. I remember sitting on the end of a diving board that we all assumed was anchored to the pier. Doug and my little brother, Clint, unbeknownst to them, were operating as my counterweight as they sat on the other end of the board. When they stood, I fell crashing into the water. I did not know how to swim.

I remember seeing Clint and Melody standing on the bank with their mouths open, stricken by fear. As I bobbed up and down in the murky waters, it felt as though the bottom dwelling weeds were wrapping themselves around my ankles and pulling me under. Suddenly, there was a large splash close to me and I felt a long, strong arm wrap around my neck and clutch my chest. It was Doug, and he had dove in to save me! I put my complete trust in Doug, and immediately stopped thrashing. He was my life saver, and knew just what to do.

Soon after, I learned how to swim. But how do you thank someone for saving your life? For me, it was an easy decision. Up until this point in my life, I was like everyone else who communicated with Doug. We would write notes and point to things. There were only a few people who could really carry on a conversation with Doug, and I decided I was going to add my name to that small list. I learned to speak using sign language (ASL).

Several years later, when Melody married and moved away, I took over as Doug's interpreter during the church services we attended. I was never as proficient as she was, but I was best suited for the job. In 2008, Doug got married and moved to Missouri. It was now 2013, and other than the credit union I worked at in Kentucky, I had few opportunities to speak using ASL.

This brings us to the ever important phone call that changed my family's life.

Riinnnnnggg....

It was Nadine, and she called to tell us about a sweet puppy who just so happened to be deaf. Where we interested?

The thought of having a deaf dog was very intriguing to us. I felt like we could do it, but in light of recent events, the call could not have come at a worse time. We were almost set to move into our farmhouse. Would it be fair to bring the puppy into our current home, only to move him again a few days later? Would he be able to adapt to his surroundings? Being deaf, would he understand? There were many questions to be answered.

It was a Friday evening, and about three weeks since the initial phone call had been received about the puppy. We were making the short drive to Portland for supper. Nadine had asked about this little puppy several times, but each time it was an emphatic "no" from me. It was just bad timing. We were still entertaining the idea, and it was on that drive that I began to pose questions about our decision.

"What if someone takes him home and cannot communicate with him? He'll be in a dark and lonely place." I thought. "What if the family that takes him gets frustrated with him and sends him to a shelter? This could happen several times and he would never trust anyone! What if he ends up in a kill shelter, and through no fault of his own he is euthanized, all because he is deaf?

That last question caused my "allergies" to act up.

Ok, truthfully, I started crying. I turned to look out my driver's side window, wiping the tears from my eyes and trying desperately to keep from showing my emotions. Tammy, already ahead of me, was texting Nadine. "What is this girl's number? Craig is crying about this puppy we've never even seen. We have to get him!"

We called the breeder, and four hours after our conversation we were pulling into a muddy gravel driveway. We parked beside a grey, worn down, single wide mobile home. Tammy and I walked up to the door and knocked while the kids stayed in the SUV. We were received into the home of a couple in their early 20's. The place wasn't well kept, and the living room had very little furniture; two non-matching cushioned chairs. The room had essentially been converted into a carpeted kennel for their dogs.

The pup's mother was the biggest boxer I had ever seen. She looked more like a small massif, but with all the proper markings of a boxer. After acclimating ourselves to our surroundings, and being greeted by this polar bear of a momma, Tammy and I looked into a corner of the carpeted kennel. There he was, laying in the corner looking lonely and confused. Just a couple of weeks ago there had been a litter of siblings to play with, but people kept whisking them away. Now he was the only one left.

"He's had a lot of people interested in him, but..." The young ladies voice trailed off.

"Can we see him?" Tammy inquired.

"Sure!" the girl said as she walked toward him. His ears perked up and his little nub tail began to wag. She picked him up and brought him to us. I took him first.

I held that little pup for less than two seconds before he nestled his head into my neck, as if to give me a hug. He just couldn't seem to get close enough. I looked longingly at Tammy. My "allergies" were acting up again. Tammy took him from me and instantly he snuggled in close to her. It was most definitely a hug! From that point on I knew I had to have him. The breeder could have charged us $3K and I would have found a way to get her the money. He was going home with us!

We stepped outside the trailer to find four faces pressed against the glass of our white SUV. Watching us step carefully from one muddy stone to the next, they could scarcely contain their excitement. We made them sit down and buckle up for the short ride home.

I placed a thin, multi-colored chevron collar around his neck and adjusted the fit. He did not like that one bit! The first five minutes of our ride home he batted at his throat trying to free himself from the vice. He eventually quit fighting and gave in. Then, fascination came over him as he looked out the windows at the world passing by faster than he had ever seen.

One of the kids declared, "Thank goodness he likes to ride in cars!" That was a true statement, for we enjoy traveling as a family. It is almost impossible to know whether a pet is a good travel companion until you take them on a "test drive". The fact is, we were already committed to this puppy, and thankfully this puppy was loving this ride to his new home!

We had a small driveway at our current house. We used it some, but we typically parked in front of the house on the street. With the SUV parked, and the pups ride over, I set him down on the ground and held his leash to see how he would navigate our steps. He was not a fan.

He followed the kids to the bottom of the steps and watched them walk up to the front door. He knew what he had to do, but decided on another tactic. He pawed the wooden steps a couple of times, let out a growl, a whimpered bark, and finally set down to wine. It worked.

"Awe, Craig. Pick him up." Tammy responded with a sweet motherly tone in her voice. I carried him into the house and took off his leash.

Our four children slapped the floor in attempts to get his attention. The pour pup was pummeled with a volley of toys deflecting off his body like a pinball machine. For the next two hours, the children surrounded him and begged to be the center of his attention.

"Let me hold him!"

"You had your turn! It's my turn now!"

"Mo-o-om! He's not giving me a turn!"

"Stop holding him so tight!"

"Give him to me!"

The precious little puppy was dazed and confused when Tammy came to his rescue. She swooped in and picked him up, then sat down in her favorite chair. With a mother's outstretched hand, she warded off all advances to get his attention. Within five minutes he was asleep in her lap.

From the music room, Isaac our oldest son, began his daily routine of hammering the drums. By now it was after 8 o'clock, which meant he had less than half an hour to practice.

"Isaac, stop banging those drums! You're going to wake the puppy!" I yelled from the living room..

The revelation hit me just as the words left my mouth. Those drums were not going to bother him at all, for the puppy could not hear. We all burst out laughing.

"Go ahead son," I said. "Play on."

## CHAPTER 2 - ENABLED

We finally had a nice place to live. The house was of a great size and had a nice, big living room. However, the 250 acres of land behind the house was the coolest part. Having access to the place meant that we could utilize the 100 acres of corn for epic hide and seek games. Having to climb the stairs to the top floor with groceries in hand was made easier because of all of the trees, the fields, and the small apple orchard that our family enjoyed. We had to use those stairs every time we went to and from work, when the kids went to school, and well...you get the point.

Stomper, the growing puppy, was being house trained. This meant frequent trips up and down the stairs. What was most inconvenient was the fact that Stomper was afraid of those stairs. To this day I do not know why he was so afraid, but if he was to make it outside in time to prevent an accident, he had to be carried.

We always attached a leash to him when we went out. Although he was not a fan, it seemed to give him a bit of confidence when going back up the stairs. After about a week in the new house, he finally built up enough courage to climb a few steps at a time. I figured it was a good start.

Stomper had now been with us for a few weeks. We were trying not to force a bunch of new things on him all at once. We thought that taking him away from his mother, and then moving him to our new house was enough for the time being. It had been an unpleasant time for us, and we could voice our concerns and opinions to each other. Stomper could not. We had made the decision to bond with him first, then teach.

Tammy is a phenomenal cook! She is the type of cook that has trouble sharing her recipes because she can simply open the pantry doors, grab a handful of food items, and thirty minutes later you are sitting at the table eating her "slap-yo-momma-good" supper! I remind the kids often that they owe me a debt of gratitude for finding the talented mother that I gave them. We decided early on in our marriage that she would be a stay-at-home mom. I would work, supporting our family monetarily. I say "we decided", but truthfully it was decided for us.

We were married September 26, 1998 in my hometown of Eminence, Kentucky. I was working at a local factory while she worked as a CNA (Certified Nursing Assistant) at the nearby hospital. She was also attending school to be an RN. We were both making "good" money, and we had a 10 year plan to take over the world like most young couples do. However, two months after we were married, all that changed.

Tammy and I had, to some extent, a weekend marriage. I worked 10 hour shifts at night, while she worked 12 hour days from 7AM to 7PM. We had ten minutes in the morning to talk, then she would leave for work while I went to bed. I was up and working before she got home, so our evenings together were nonexistent.

While on her way to work one morning in mid-November, Tammy was at the backend of a small line of traffic. A few vehicles in front of her, a water district truck was turning into a residency to read their meter. The driveway was narrow, so the truck had to turn in slowly. Tammy and a small pickup truck in front of her had to come to a complete stop. Coming at them from behind was a young seventeen year old boy driving over 55 MPH on that winding, country road. He was enjoying his newly installed stereo and had taken his eyes off the road. When he finally looked up, it was too late. Tammy watched her rearview mirror in horror as the agonizing sounds of screeching tires was followed by a low rumbling thud as fiberglass and metal collided with her car. His car slammed into Tammy with such force that she was sandwiched between the truck in front of her and his pickup. We later learned that, surprisingly, it was the young boy's fifth wreck in just one year!

In that single moment, whiplash, disc misalignment, and muscle tears caused by the full-forced front and rear impacts would cost Tammy her job and also the career she had planned for. She still deals with the injuries she suffered that day, and that is the foremost reason she was now a stay-at-home mom.

We had now been married for 14 years, had four kids, and a dog who was blessed to have us together with him in his human home. Well, most of the time. When we were not home, Stomper would stay in a large metal kennel that had plenty of room for him to play. As long as he was close to a window he did fairly well with it. The kennel really helped us house break him too.

At night, Stomper did not want to be in his kennel, but wanted to be wherever the kids were sleeping. Because we all slept on the same floor in the new house, and their beds were low to the floor, he was free to move around and snuggle up to whomever he chose. I would take him out to potty right before bedtime and he would wait until morning before he went again. He was perfect!

It must have been around 9AM on a Saturday morning. I was awake but lying on the right side of my bed with my hand dangling off the side, when I felt sharp pins jabbing into my pinky.

"Ow!" I squealed as I yanked my hand back. I looked to the floor to see what had attacked me. It was Stomper. I hung my hand over the side again to see what he would do. He bit me again! Believing that he was playing too rough, I pointed at him and called him a bad boy, then rolled over so he could not reach me anymore. I could hear his paws as they rustled on the carpet, reached onto the bed, then rustled back again onto the floor.

"Maybe he's trying to tell you something." Tammy urged. "Follow him."

Reluctantly, I put both feet on the floor as Tammy and I snickered about Stomper's breathing getting faster as I moved in his direction. I lowered my hand down to where Stomper could reach it, and what happened next was a pivotal moment in our journey together. Stomper clasped my hand between his teeth for the third time and began walking with a bit of a strut as his bobbed tail wagged behind him. I walked crouched over with my pinky held tightly between those needle like puppy teeth to the front door, about twenty feet away from my bed. My wife followed.

Stomper's leash was hanging on the doorknob. To our amazement, little Stomper stopped right in front of the door, let go of my hand, and stood there with his chest puffed out in pride. He was breathing so fast, and I'm sure I could see a smile on his face because of his accomplishment. Me? Well, my allergies were acting up!

I was overjoyed! Stomper was communicating with us! He needed to be let outside, so he came to get me to make it happen. We talked about it all through breakfast and decided it was time to teach. Stomper needed to be taught sign language.

American Sign Language uses hand gestures to symbolize letters in the English language. Often, the words spoken in ASL are the creation of shapes for those words. For example, the word "house" is signed by touching the tips of both hands together at an angle and forming the shape of a rooftop, then holding the hands parallel to each other to symbolize the sides of the house. How hard could it be to teach a dog some of these signs? I could not answer that question because none of us in my family had ever seen that attempted before, but this little puppy was smart and eager to learn.

The problem with training Stomper was that he would rather run off and play instead of focusing his attention on my hands. He was afraid of stairs, and because of this we had never tried to put him in high places. The only solution I could think of was to put him up onto our bed. There he would be a captive audience and I could get his attention better. Our bed was a king size bed that was much higher off the floor, and a smaller kid would even have to get a running start to get on it. I picked Stomper up, and placed him on the high surface, then knelt down at the foot of the bed to be closer to eye-level with him.

The wrinkles on his forehead were that of concern as I set him on the bed. He was a little freaked out because he had never been on the bed, but I never left his side. I petted and loved on him until he calmed down. Tammy had the idea of using cheese crackers to incentivize him. I had never trained a dog before so I was willing to give it a shot. They could not have worked better!

I began to work methodically through the process. His first trick would be to sit on command. I placed my hands on either side of his face about a foot away so his eyes could not wonder. I extended my middle and index fingers on both hands and gently tapped the back of my left hand with the extended fingers of my right. "Sit" I said, then pushed his bottom down. That was met with a lot of puppy power resistance!

Stomper did not know what to think of this game. He fought me for a short bit, but finally set on the bed. While holding his backside down, I fed him a cheese cracker and loved on him for a moment. I removed my hand from his bottom and he stood right back up, and I began the process again. Sign, force the position, and a treat with positive attention. We did this a couple of times when suddenly, a lightbulb went off in his head. I showed him the sign, and it happened. Stomper sat! I was in shock, but gave him two cheese crackers to celebrate!

Up until this point, Tammy and the kids had been banned from the room so as not to be a distraction, but I called them in. They piled in to watch. I gestured for Stomper to sit, but of course he did not want to. Was Stomper going to choke under the pressure of an audience, or was he too distracted?

Tammy offered a suggestion, "Put a Cheez-It in your hand when you sign to him." So I showed him the crackers and immediately I had his attention. His eyes would not leave my hands, so I signed for him to sit and he set. The kids went crazy! They cheered and clapped as Stomper ate his new favorite snack.

"Try to get him to lay down," Tammy suggested. So I opened my left palm and turned it upward, then extended the thumb and first two fingers of my right hand outward with palm up. As I said the word "lay", I slapped my right hand down onto my left hand. I then quickly pulled his front legs out from under him, forcing him to lay down. That little forehead crinkled up again. The concern quickly faded with the revealing of another Cheez-It. He sat up again and ate it. So again I signed for him to lay and reached for his front legs, but this time he laid himself down!

A chorus of laughter and shouts of, "No way" was all that could be heard in that bedroom. My entire family had just witnessed our precious baby learning a language allowing us to communicate with him. So I taught them the signs, and one by one they would either sign "lay" or "sit" with a Cheez-It in their hand. They were mesmerized at how smart our newest family edition was! Over the next few days we worked with him, teaching him signs like "bathroom", and even how to "fist bump."

The most transformational part about all of this was not the confirmation that we had made the right choice to bring Stomper home, or that we were learning to communicate with him, or witnessing how he could communicate with us. Stomper was gaining confidence! As a two month old puppy, Stomper was very quiet with no confidence at all. If one of us left a room, he had to be directly at our feet. He was afraid of the stairs, and for obvious reasons afraid of the dark. But after being in the Hedge's household for a while, as long as he could see into a couple of rooms, he would pick out his own favorite places to play and lie down. He even began to navigate the stairs all on his own! He did not have to follow us everywhere, afraid that he would miss something. Stomper was becoming confident!

Language is a funny thing. If you have ever been anywhere, in a crowded room or a new place where you did not know the language well, you can empathize with the disconnected feeling you have with the environment. Even those who exude poise and self-assurance will struggle to fit in with a culture that speaks a different language. Many pity Stomper because of his absents of sound. Comments like "poor baby" and "bless his heart" are often used when people find out that Stomper is deaf. It is difficult for some people to perceive that life can be fulfilling even though some may not be able to do what they can do. The truth is, regardless of your lot in life, happiness can be found!

Helen Keller once said, "When one door of happiness closes, another opens; but often we look so long at the closed door that we do not see the one which has been opened for us."

We did not find a "family pet" when we first met that shy, white puppy with the sad eyes, droopy jaws, and wrinkled forehead. Instead, life had united us with a new member of our family that would prove to be challenging at times. But more than that, he would teach us that our differences are what brings about balance to our lives. Stomper was showing us a better way to love!

## CHAPTER 3 - FORGIVENESS

A major part of having a dog in your house (or any other animal) is the responsibility that goes along with it. Establishing a "potty" schedule that works for you as well as them, is top priority. Also, do they have enough food? What about food that is beneficial to them? Do you work away from home? What does that schedule look like?

Tammy being a stay-at-home mom was instrumental in getting Stomper on a regular routine. She would take him for walks to "relieve" himself. But because Tammy is so small, if our growing puppy saw a bird or similar distraction, he would go after it causing Tammy to have to plant her feet and really lean back on the leash to keep from being dragged to whatever grabbed Stomper's attention. Several times this caused rope burn on Tammy's hands. We figured out that by keeping a little tension on his leash it was a constant reminder that we were on the other end. It helped in keeping him from getting lost in the moment, and kept us from being dragged through the grass.

He was not a fan of the leash, but it was a necessity because we lived on a busy road. River Road is curvy, matching the river that runs along its length. If traveling westbound on River Road, cars would have difficulty spotting Stomper. Because we could not call out to him, it took a while to teach him to stop. We accomplished this by teaching him that two tugs on the rope meant for him to stop and look to us for communicative instructions. With Stomper, the leash was absolutely necessary.

We noticed early on that Stomper's sense of sight and smell were incredible, uncommonly more than in other dogs we had owned. Around our house set the 250 acres of farmland, with most of the cropland laying behind our house and over a small hill. The only way to access it was by going through a gate, then walking or driving the half mile to the back. I cannot count how many adventurous tripped we took back through the farm. To the west end of the house lay about 50 acres of corn crop. As it grew taller visibility diminished, but that did not deter Stomper from pointing and growling at whatever was out there. We never saw another animal out there, but with Stomper's senses, I never doubted those growls.

Not everyone in our family was "authorized" to take Stomper out. He was too strong for the two younger boys and they might have been hurt but for the most part Stomper was no trouble. He was terrific about letting you know he needed to go outside. Also, if he needed more food or water, he would walk to where one of us was (usually Tammy) and take a few steps back toward his bowl, then return to her. Intuitively, he knew that by communicating with his family, he would have every need met.

If Stomper needed to burn off some energy, we could take him to the back fields and let him loose for a bit. It was safely located away from the road and once back there we could unfasten him from the leash. The huge fields were perfect for our growing puppy to exhaust himself. The only problem was catching him when it was time to head back to the house.

Living on the second level of the 4,000 sq ft farmhouse had its benefits, but we needed to barricade the hallway to insure the chandelier in the apartment below us did not fall on our neighbor's kitchen table. One of the benefits was the view. We had the most perfect tree sitting right in front of our bedroom window, and it was beautiful in every season. Just beyond the tree was the road, followed by a 30 foot rocky descent to a river bed. The river was wide, and above that rocky descent was a thick, gorgeous tree line. The view was incredible! The noise however, was a bit of an issue.

About a mile from our house, on the opposite side of the river, was a distribution center for a big box store. During the day you could hear cars buzzing by, but at night it was the beep, beep, beep of those trucks at the distribution center.

We would often hike the trail behind the house because of its serene beauty. It was fairly steep going up the hill, but the view while hiking was beautiful. If you made it to the top, you were rewarded with a breathtaking view. The view consisted of a large corn patch to the left, and to the right was a patch of woods. There was a well-manicured piece of ground in the middle, and if you were brave enough, you could continue on to the back hill which was perfect for sledding in the winter. In autumn, the trees became most every color imaginable. This was our playground!

Sometimes we would drive back on the property and take footballs and kick balls to play with. The area was great for throwing frisbees, and we had the most epic hide and seek games in the cornfield. I had a secret to always winning! It was not until after we moved that I told the kids how I always won those hide and seek games. I shared how I would go out into the field, count to 50, and then....stand still. For the next moment I would simply listen for Stomper's collar to jingle. From there it was just a matter of following my ears. Stomper has always been the most curious dog and he would sniff out each kid to see where they were going. That is how I always won.

Some of the best pictures of Stomper as a puppy were taken back on that far ridge. Sometimes our growing pup would just sit in the sunshine and enjoy himself, and other times he wanted to run. We taught him to chase balls that we threw, but he would never bring them back to us. He would master that skill as he got older.

One afternoon the sun arose with very few clouds in the sky. I wanted to get a few pictures of Stomper, so I walked him out to the fields by myself. He was calmer than usual because it was just the two of us. I took some exceptional shot with my camera phone that day, but one in particular made me most proud. The picture itself was good, but the sacrifice it took to actually take the shot makes me laugh every time I think about it.

It was hard that day to get a shot of Stomper from a distance. He was excitable and always wanted to stay close to me. Even in that wide open field he would run away from you only to a certain distance, then glance around and make sure he could still see you. For this picture, I caught him lying in the grass paying no attention to me, and quickly ran in the direction I needed to frame the shot. I crouched down into the grass to get an eye level view, and when he saw me he immediately ran in my direction. I pushed the camera button repeatedly on my phone as fast as I could to try and get the best facial expressions he would make. I was not expecting what happened next. Stomper, in a full run straight at me, had no plans of stopping. He slammed full throttle into my phone knocking it from my hands, and the phone quickly found my surprised face. Following that was Stomper, and he plowed into me like a hay bale rolling down a hill.

I do not fall easily! I am a broad shouldered man with short legs which gives me a very low center of gravity. It just wasn't enough. I was knocked off my haunches into the grass, which dazed me for a second. I jumped to my feet and immediately looked around to see if anyone saw my fall. I burst out laughing!

I picked up my phone from the ground and turned to see if Stomper was alright. He was sitting a few feet away from me with the most worried look that I've ever seen on a dog's face. He was genuinely concerned with whether or not he hurt me, so I knelt down on my knees and called for him to come to me. He was timid, but came on over. I petted him and hugged him, and because it was often a chore to catch him in the fields, I went ahead and leashed him up to head back to the house.

I made a mental note that day about the growing strength of our newest family member. I gathered the family around when I got home to tell them of my exploits and to explain my new grass stains. It was the perfect time to reiterate our rule that only four of the six of us could take Stomper out to the bathroom. If he could knock "big daddy" over, then the rest of them were certainly capable of getting hurt. Stomper was so strong as a pup that his muscular legs had, at some point, dragged Tammy to the ground, pulled Hannah down the last few stairs in the front yard, and bruised Isaac a time or two as he tried to keep Stomper from chasing a bird out of "his" tree. Our two youngest boys, Ian and Eli, were certainly not capable of handling the strength and solid mass of our 6-month old beast of a puppy.

Several weeks had past and Maine was just entering into its rainy season. Since all of the kids were now in school it made sense for Tammy to go back to work on a part-time basis. She had found a job at a local retail store that was willing to work with the hours she needed to be home not long after the kids were dropped off from the bus. Our downstairs neighbor, Pauline, was almost always home and loved our kids. This gave us some peace of mind as well. On this day Tammy and I were working, but the kids were home on a holiday from school. We invited the kid's cousin over to stay with them and to keep them under control while we were gone. Kasee would spend the night and we figured she could help reinforce the rules we expected to be followed. She was a couple of years older than our oldest child and daughter, Hannah. Tammy and I had already left for work and it was raining that morning, which was typical for the season. We worked out a plan and the details were to call the kids periodically to make sure they were doing ok. There was just one small problem. The girls stayed up so late talking that they did not wake up until late morning.

It was mid-morning before I was made aware by the news of what happened. It came in the form of a text from

Tammy, followed by a picture of our eight year old son, Ian, who was not on our authorized list of family members who could take Stomper outside.

It happened somewhere in the morning around 9 o'clock when Stomper needed to go outside. All the kids were asleep but Isaac, who was doing his own thing, and Ian. Ian was working on his typical morning routine of grabbing a quick breakfast and then picking up where he left of the night before in one of his books. Stomper came by and nudged Ian, so he tried waking the girls up to let them know Stomper needed out. He was met by moans and groans from the girls, so he told Isaac. Isaac mentioned that they were to stay in the house. Ian needed to act now. There was urgency on his friends face!

Ian has a heart like his mother. It is a mystery how that big ol' heart can fit in such a small chest. His concern for Stomper's urgent need to tinkle outside, superseded his warning to say put inside. He showed no regard for the fact that he was not on the authorized list to take Stomper out because his friend was in need! Ian grabbed the leash, hooked up his excited buddy and headed down the stairs to the side of the house. Although there was no rain just then, there was an overhanging of murky clouds that looked as though they could burst at any time.

Stomper went through the same ritual every time he was taken out to potty. The first couple of steps in the grass were done with is head held high, sniffing for any intruder that may have wondered off track and into his territory. If all was to his liking he would then sniff the ground in a patterned path, returning to a random spot that was somehow the chosen place, and then do his business. Ian was careful to keep tension on the leash throughout the whole ritual.

Without warning the clouds above broke and it started raining. The first drop of water to hit Stomper on the back caused him to spin around violently to find his would be attacker. But there was no one there. Then the second drop hit along with a hundred others. He was in a frenzy and didn't know what to do. Nervously, Ian was trying to console him with words to no avail. Stomper could not hear him.

There are several large boulders beside our parking area that separate the farm land from our residential plot. There was space enough to walk between them and they made great hide and seek spots. Maybe that is why Stomper chose to run in that direction instead of through the open door of the house. The rain was gaining momentum and Stomper leapt out toward the rocks. Ian who still had hold of the leash, ran behind Stomper as he surged behind the largest of the boulders looking for shelter. As Stomper dragged Ian, the boy's leg hit the side of the big boulder. Never mind, Ian was not letting go of the rope! All he could think of was Stomper running into the road and getting hurt or killed. Ian just refused to let go of the leash.

From his new vantage point behind one of the boulders, Stomper peered through the pouring rain. He spied the open door to the house just a dash away and he bolted!

As Stomper dashed toward safety, Ian's little legs could not keep up. Like a kite in the wind, he was dragged toward the house. The landing just outside the door is made of naturally rough, unyielding stone. Stomper leaped through the air, cleared the stone and landed in the open doorway. Suddenly the leash went tight around Stomper's neck. Ian, still holding the taught leash, was thrust into the air and face planted into the white wood trim that edged the side of the house. It was not until Stomper was safely in the hallway and away from harm that Ian finally let go. It was a little too late and the damage done. Ian blacked out for a moment as he set on the wet stone. He was drenched in rain and now bleeding profusely from his head.

Although Stomper was free to run because nothing was holding him back, he turned back to Ian sensing that something was wrong with his buddy. He sat in the doorway worrying and refusing to leave his friend, but not knowing exactly what to do. He was concerned, and seemed to know this was his fault. Ian stood shakily to his feet and began to climb the stairs with Stomper right at his side. His left eye was beginning to swell and he did not know where all the blood was coming from, but he knew he was hurt. He limped into the house crying, and Isaac ran to wake the girls.

Hannah rushed Ian into the bathroom to help stop the bleeding and clean him up, while Kasee called Tammy. Tammy rushed home. She rushed into the house and to her relief found that most of the bleeding had stopped. She began to assess Ian's injuries, and although his leg was ok, his face was not. His left eye was swollen badly and was cut up from contact with the corner of the house. Although Hannah had done a good job of cleaning Ian's face, there were still paint flecks in his hairline and around the cuts. There was a deep gash about an inch above his eyebrow that would require further medical attention.

All through the traumatic situation, Stomper never left Ian's side. With his bobbed tail tucked tightly under his backside and his floppy ears glued to his head, he followed Tammy to the door as she left to take Ian to the hospital. When they left, he sat by the door waiting. He was worried.

I hurriedly met them at the ER. Although Ian was in a lot of pain, the first thing he did was explain to me that Stomper was not to blame. He was taking up for his buddy.

"Dad, it wasn't Stomper's fault. I shouldn't have taken him out. The rain just freaked him out!."

I inquiringly asked, "Why didn't you just let go of the leash buddy?"
Ian bravely replied, "Because I was afraid he'd run toward the road, and I needed to protect him."

My allergies were acting up again.

A kind nurse came in asking what had happened. After explaining the situation, she told us about a product called a Gentle Leader. Apparently, she had a large German Shepherd who had done a similar thing to one of her kids. "My 5 year old can lead him around now. He just doesn't pull." We bought a Gentle Leader that afternoon! The medical staff cleaned Ian's wounds, used an adhesive to close the gash, and then put a few butterfly bandages on it.

When we arrived home, Stomper was still waiting for us by the door. He looked worried as the three of us entered the house. The kids rumbled the floor as they flew in to the kitchen to find out what Ian looked like. We talked to the kids explaining what the doctor and nurses had done, and then had a brief discussion on how we were going to prevent further occurrences of this sort. Stomper just sat there, never moving. The siblings exited the kitchen leaving the three of us behind with a puppy too petrified to move.

Ian slowly walked toward Stomper. The puppy's breathing changed and he started to pant heavily through his nose. Ian crouched down in front of Stomper, and reaching out, gave him a big hug. Stomper went into a big, full-bodied wag as his whole body shook. It was as if a burdening load was lifted from him in that moment. Ian cheerfully stood and limped into the living room. Now it was mom and dad that Stomper faced. We knelt down and Stomper slowly walked into our arms as we hugged him.

I've heard it said that, "Forgiveness is for the forgiver, more than who is being forgiven." To a point that is true, but sometimes walls are built in the mind of the offender because they believe themselves to be beyond forgiveness. They cannot imagine anyone forgiving them for what they have done. Therefore walls are built on both sides. I believe that forgiveness is for all parties involved. However, it is up to the individual what they do with the gift of forgiveness and how they let it impact their life and relationships.

Do you have walls? I'm sure you do. We've all built them at some point, but what are you going to build next? Will it be a moat or a bridge? That choice is yours to make.

## CHAPTER 4 - LOVE UNCONDITIONAL

Winter is a season in Maine that is either loved or hated, but if you have the snow gear it is a playground of fun! The slopes are full of skiers and snowboarders looking to hit the fresh powder after a night of snowfall. The beauty of everything covered in white making all things equal, was somewhat tranquil. Expensive cars cannot be distinguished from clunkers in a parking lot, and people bundle themselves so completely that nationalities appear unknown. I loved the snow!

Many people hated the winters there. Folks who lived there since birth were less enthusiastic about it as I was. I would listen to them grumble for a bit, then remind them that there was opportunity to live in 49 other states in this great country. The conversations usually ended with a laugh, but rarely continued past that. The part of snow that I never got used to was the period right after a good snowfall.

In Kentucky we had snow, but it was nothing compared to where we were living in Maine. The greatest defining difference was the temperature. Snowfalls in Kentucky usually happen in 20 degree weather, not sub-zero temperatures! In a 20 degree snowfall there is a clumping factor that makes for great snowballs, which means great snowball fights! When the ground is frozen solid in sub-zero temperatures, the snow fall is like a powder, completely susceptible to the wind. When a good stiff wind blew across the surface of the snowdrifts it would carry the top layer back into the air in a horizontal direction. If you were to walk outside when the powder is riding the wind there is a strong chance that a few flakes of snow would drive themselves directly into your ear canals. There is no feeling like it in the world! I did not realize I had nerve endings that deep inside my skull. There is no cure for this sensation that causes your brain to scream from the inside, and every time I encountered it I would instantly become angry: hulk like angry!

"Just wear a hat," people would say through their laughter as they listened to me rant about the pain in my ear holes.

"I don't look right in a hat," I would always explain. If you can go far enough back to remember black and white tv, imagine me looking like Beaver Cleaver. I have this big round head, and I am sure that's why all baseball caps say "One Size Fits Most".

"How about ear muffs," they might suggest. "Well if I ever find any that allows me to sustain a certain level of manliness then maybe," I'd reply. Maine was more about function rather than fashion, and I never caught on.

The first good snowfall with Stomper living in our house hit in December, 2013. It was not enough to cover the top of the grass as blades still protruded from underneath, but it changed the atmosphere and certainly put us in the mood for Christmas. How would Stomper react to seeing snow for the first time?

The amount of snowfall that fell overnight was not going to stop us from getting out and enjoying our Saturday morning. The frigid sub-zero wind chills, well that was another thing entirely. After testing nature, we decided to "hangout" inside, at least until the sun warmed the temperatures up a bit. We were cleaning up from breakfast when Stomper started barking and growling like we had never heard before. Pawing at the kitchen window from the second level, Stomper was anxious to get outside. Tammy, thinking maybe a fox or a stray dog had wandered into the yard, walked over to see what the commotion was all about.

"Craig, get in here! There's a moose in the front yard!"

All six of us ran into the kitchen, nearly trampling one another to huddle around the front window as Stomper continued to bark and the moose crossed the road into our neighbor's yard. Although his head was eye level with the door frame of the house across the road, we were told by family who watched the video we captured of him that he was a young moose. He loped around the house and into a line of trees toward the river. We were so excited to see him! To this day that is the only moose we've ever seen outside of game farms and zoos. How did Stomper sense him first? Did he smell something in the air that we could not? Did he happen to look out the window at just the right time?

There were so many moments that winter which made me rethink what "normal" was. Many nights we would take him out into the cold and he would growl at some unforeseen thing. You just knew something was out there by the intense, guttural growl which Stomper emitted. From the nape of his neck to his bobbed tail, Stomper would grow a 3 inch wide Mohawk along his back as he bristled. With snow on the ground it was all quiet except for the occasional car going by. The farm was full of wildlife and sometimes he would get so unnerved that it would take everything in us to keep him from charging the would be intruder. I have always heard that if one sense is missing that the other senses will make up the difference. That concept was never more clear to me than with Stomper. If someone slammed a door, he could be at the opposite end of the house and he would jump up and run to see who it was. In his mind, he was quickly taking on the role as family protector.

Every time we came home Stomper would march around the entire house checking the rooms for potential threats, as if he was the only thing between our safety and certain death. We dubbed him the "White Centurion" because of his diligence to prance around the house upon our return and peer out every window, making his presence known with a guttural growl to ward off potential threats. Only then was he satisfied to greet us with tail wags, body leans, and paws that often left their marks on our skin. We developed quite the routine, and by maintaining a schedule it was easier for him to accept us leaving because we scheduled our returns to the house around the same times.

Maine's seasons were as distinct as the local's accents. Nature left no doubt when the seasons changed. Winter was coming to a close and had not been horrible that year. The cold was dreadful but we lived on a busy road and realized we were top priority when the road crew cleared the snowfalls. In Maine it is often said that there are 5 seasons: spring, summer, fall, winter, and mud. The muddy season is when all the leftover snow begins to melt and overflows the rivers, saturating the ground. If you have an ATV, it's the best time of the year.

Spring was in the air. We had survived another winter followed by a relatively mild muddy season. The snow had melted away and now buds were on the trees. The path to the back of the farm was finally clearing up and Stomper was more than aware that the energy he had pent up over the winter was about to find its outlet. The leash pulling started again. It had taken a few weeks for Ian's head to heal from his and Stomper's rain incident, and only a couple of months for Stomper to forget about it all together.

Birds began nesting in the trees and landing in the yard. He could not help but give chase, but this time we had our "Gentle Leader" which prevented him from pulling us, regardless of how hard he tried. He would give the leash good tug, remember he was wearing his new harness, and then let out a big sigh of disgust as he sat helplessly watching the intruders go about their day in his yard. Occasionally however, he got loose. We were constantly reminding the kids to close the doors behind them, but inevitably someone would forget. If they did forget, he would run down the stairs, through the hallway behind the garage and out the side door. This would suspend the next ten to fifteen minutes of our lives chasing our small "horse" all over the side field and often into the front yard. Of course it was always when we had somewhere else to be.

The front yard was especially dangerous. It was well manicured with a couple of small trees on either side of a white poplar tree that was so photogenic in every season that it was common to look out our front window and see drivers pulling over to take pictures of our magnificent spectacle. It was quite the spectacle and plenty of people got to see it because of its location near the road. The busy road allowed plenty of visitors access to enjoy it. It stood more than 60 feet tall and had no competition around it to contest its beauty. The heavy traffic would not allow us to entrust the kids to the front yard, and it was used mostly to try and catch Stomper when he got loose.

On more than one occasion Stomper would run across the road in a rather frightening game of tag. It was Isaac who would often run away from him as if he were "it", coaxing him away from the road. As Stomper would rush in, Isaac would tackle him. Those days where the good times, but on this day it did not turn out as well.

Stomper had run across the road back and forth about 4 times already. He was in the side field being chased by several of us when he darted for the road yet again. I had stood in the street and waved the traffic to a slower speed, but they would just blow their horns as Stomper sped by. What good was that because he could not hear?

This time Stomper ran completely across the road and down the embankment. The cars going by could not see him until he popped up to dart back across the road in front of them. That's when it happened. We watched in horror as Stomper ran right out in front of a driver. The man mashed his brake pedal, locking his tires up and coming to a screeching to a halt. We heard a heart-stopping yelp amidst the screeching tires as Stomper's body spun around from the impact. His ears dropped back as he realized for the first time that he was in any kind of danger. Stomper had been hit by a car!

The man driving the car was shaken up and jumped out, not caring about the traffic. I was running toward the scene from the field as Stomper hobbled over to us. I thanked the man for stopping and he said, "I thought it was a ghost dog!" The man was clearly shaken, realizing that he had just hit someone's family member. If he had not stopped the way he did, I'm not sure how bad it would have been and for that I am forever grateful to that man. But, "Ghost Dog"?

Tammy took Stomper to the veterinarian and explained the situation. Stomper's hip was bruised but he would be ok. The vet warned her that there could be some long term effects that might creep up over time, but the real concern was a tendon behind his knee. When the car clipped him Stomper's ACL was ripped, but not torn through completely. He could not put any weight on his leg, so now we had a 78 lb. dog that could neither walk up or down the stairs to go anywhere, and would have difficulty using the bathroom.

"You know what this means, right," Tammy asked on the phone as she filled me in from the vet visit.

"Yep! Hannah is going to have to carry him up and down the stairs to take him out," I responded jokingly, but somewhat hopeful.

"Uh, no. He's all yours for the next three weeks."

"Three weeks," I exclaimed.

"That's what the doctor said." Tammy went on to explain that Stomper would be taking anti-inflammatories along with some glucosamine and fish oil tablets. This would help with joint issues that the vet assured her would most definitely be coming down the road.

At home, Stomper walked to the base of the steps and lunged as though he would push through the pain, so not to inconvenience anyone. I put tension on the leash and he turned and looked at me. I put my hands around his big barreled chest and slowly lifted him. His breathing became heavy as he tried to figure out what I was doing. His head bobbed around as I lifted him, and his legs kicked and flailed for something to support himself with. I held him like that at the foot of the stairs until he stopped.

I remembered the first time I held Stomper when he nestled his head into my neck as if to hug me. This time he was facing the opposite direction, but somehow he understood I was trying to help and that he was not in as much pain. Once he realized that he was stable, I walked cautiously up the stairs with my buddy. At the top I slowly set him back down and he turned and looked at me as if to say thank you, then hobbled on into the house. This was the first of many trips up and down those stairs. Each trip got easier as Stomper realized this was his new way of life. Well, at least for a while.

The day came when Stomper was released by the doctor to start using the steps on his own. My arm and leg muscles could not have been happier! We waited a few weeks after his first solo flight up and down the stairs before we decided to take him to the back field for some exercise. He had definitely gained weight during his healing process. Hannah wanted to walk him down the path to stretch his legs, and once they were at the field she let him loose. Stomper did what he does every time; he ran.

Sometimes the boys would throw Stomper balls or a Frisbee, but today they were back there playing soccer. Stomper was running through the field on that sunny day, perfect for play. All of a sudden the boys heard a yelp. They whirled around in time to see Stomper rolling on the ground, writhing in pain. As Stomper was running, his foot had lodged in a hole, the same leg that was healing from the car wreck. They ran to him and hooked up his collar to walk him back to the house. It was a half mile trek downhill to the house and Stomper limped as he refused to put pressure on the foot.

At the base of the stairs Hannah picked him up the same way she's seen me do, but Stomper was heavy. She could only get a few steps at a time, but she finally climbed all the stairs with him in her arms. All four kids tried to be the first one to tell Tammy what had happened as they burst through the door with Stomper. He was in more pain now than ever before.

He was practically lifeless that night, and even carrying him up and down the stairs seemed to make him more restless than before. Stomper was in a lot of pain, and we went to bed knowing we would be making another trip to the vet in the morning.

It was about three o'clock in the morning when Isaac came into our bedroom. "Mom...mom...Stomper is crying, and his leg is pulled up weird. I tried to pet him and he nipped at me. I think somethings wrong."

Tammy and I got up to see our fur baby laying on his bed with a sincerely worried look on his face. His forehead was wrinkled with confusion as to what was happening, and his bobbed tail was tucked tight and his ears drawn back. Stomper was squirming on his bed trying desperately to find a comfortable position in which to rest but was unsuccessful. His breathing was labored as if he wanted to scream in pain and fear but did not know how to make the sounds come out. He did not know what was happening, but he knew the pain was unbearable.

"Craig, what should we do," Tammy asked in a panicked voice that mirrored the worried look on Stomper's face. My wife is an animal lover to the very depth of her bones. One of our first arguments was when we were dating and came across a beagle who was obviously lost and wondering around the Natchez Trace. Tammy wanted to stop and pick it up. I did not.

It wasn't as if Tammy did not know what to do, but with several options she wanted to choose just the right one that would give Stomper the fastest relief. I made the call based on a past experience I had as a thirteen year old kid.

I was taking some medication for an ear infection and the instructions were to take it twice daily until the capsules ran out. I had missed one of my nightly doses, and being a kid I decided to take two the next morning to "catch up" on the dose I had missed. That evening I started having neck and facial spasms. My neck turned my head to my left side like I was looking over my left shoulder, and my facial muscles were drawing up causing me to look like I was smiling. It would not have been such a big deal, but I was standing on the second row of the church I attended and we were right in the middle of our song service. It was our Wednesday night Bible study.

My buddy, Arnie, was standing on my left. "What are you doing? Pastor is looking at us!"

"I can't help it! My face is stuck," I said through the Joker-like smile on my lips. I went downstairs and rubbed my neck and face until my muscles relaxed and unfroze, then went back upstairs to sit with my mother. She sat further back in the sanctuary on the left side.

"What were you doing up there? My brother was staring at you," she asked. My uncle was the Pastor of our church which housed about 70 people.

"Mom, I couldn't help it. My neck turned and I couldn't stop smiling."

"Well, stay back here with me for now."

"Yes ma'am," I replied.

My uncle had read his scripture text and had just started teaching when it happened again. This time my neck drew my head upward and my mouth opened to a position that caused things to crack and pop in my jaw. I smacked my mom's leg.

Mom spoke up and interrupted her brother, "Uh, Craig is having some kind of muscle spasm. Can we pray?"

The service was essentially over at that point. I had held it in as long as I could, but now I let out a cry. I could not say anything because of the position of my mouth. So the ministry gathered around me and began to pray. This went on for about half an hour. They were crying out to God but he wasn't answering their prayers; at least not the way I wanted Him to.

Finally my uncle looked at me and said, "Craig, we've been praying for a while now. Do you want to stay and continue to pray, or do you want us to get you to a hospital?"

"Ah-Ah-Ah! Ah-Ah-Ah!" That was all I could manage to say. I am a firm believer in the power of prayer because I have seen blinded eyes opened, cancers healed, and many other miracles in my lifetime. But at that moment, I wanted to go to the hospital! That is what I was trying to say! Count the syllables: Ho-spi-tal! But that is not what my uncle heard.

"Folks, Craig's faith is strong. He wants to stay and pray."

"AH-AH-AH! AH-AH-AH!"

Fortunately there was a lady who worked in the school system who had the brilliant idea of running a couple of towels under hot water, then wrapping them around my neck and onto my face. Sure enough, the muscles relaxed in just a few minutes and I received some relief. I had one more episode that night when I got home, so I got my own towel and treated the angry muscles myself. I never doubled up on medicine again!

So when Tammy asked what I thought we should do for Stomper, the answer was easy for me. His muscles were contracting so we needed to provide relief. Hot towels. We laid a couple over his leg and hip, being careful not to get too close to him. We really weren't sure how he would react.

Finally his leg began to relax and we were able to give him some ibuprofen to help the inflammation.

It was back to the veterinarian the next day. He had torn the tendon almost completely this time. Muscle relaxers and the same treatment as before was prescribed. This time, if he did not stay off his leg as it healed we would be forced to amputate it. Those were dark words. This energetic, one-year old baby was now nearly lifeless and anything he did cause him pain. We kept meds in him throughout the whole process, but he would never completely heal.

It was now back to carrying him up and down the stairs. We stopped letting him run free in the fields behind us. It was not worth the risk of causing him any more pain should something else go wrong. Besides, he could lose his left hind leg. That was not a pleasant thought.

There is a song that says, "Love is a many splendored thing." There is a lot of truth packed into that statement. Society wants us to see love as goosebumps and heart flutters, and there is a joyous place for that, but when I think of love now I tend to lean more toward a definition like this:

Love is taking care of one another.

Sometimes it is inconvenient. Sometimes it is costly. But it is always worth it!

Stomper looks at us differently now than he did before he was hurt. It's as though he knows that when things aren't right you need to take care of the people you love. He is concerned when something is not right in the family, and he gets excited when we get excited. He has aligned his emotions with the emotions of his family because he feels love. And because he feels that unconditional love, he gives it back in abundance.

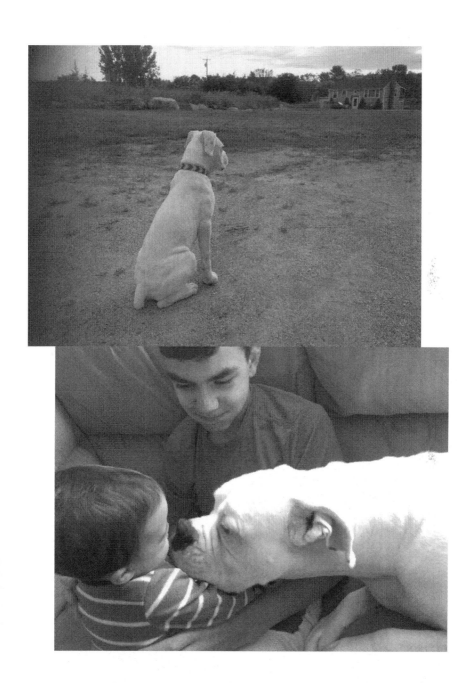

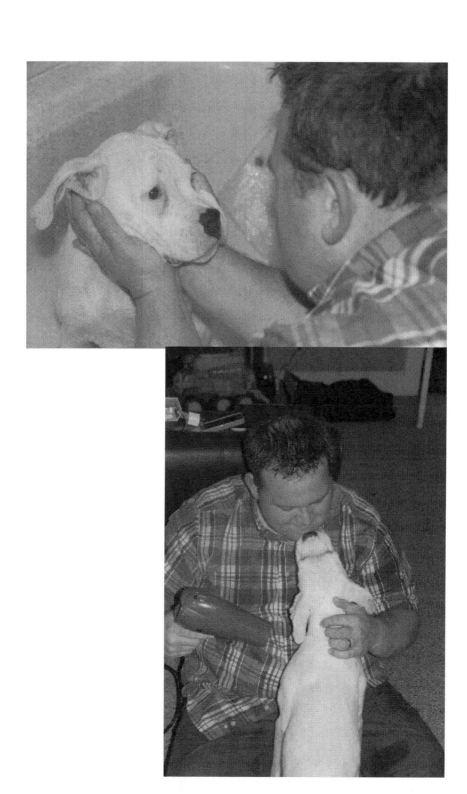

## CHAPTER 5 - CONQUERING FEAR

Living in that big farmhouse had its advantages and disadvantages. We loved the space, and even though our neighbors were nice, we disliked having to share it. There was a grandmother and daughter beneath us, and the granddaughter lived in the apartment above the three-car garage. Grandmother Pauline had a small Chihuahua, and Stephanie the granddaughter, had two pit bulls. Stomper played well with the larger dogs, but Pauline's "little barker" wouldn't have anything to do with him. Occasionally Diesel, the youngest pit, would get loose and run into our part of the house if the door was open. After ushering him back home, the kids would laugh about it for the next thirty minutes!

Pauline was a vegan. I do not know very much about the vegan lifestyle, but I do know they are healthier than I am. No member of my family can imagine doing without all the things vegans have vowed not to eat. Our determination to maintain omnivore status was solidified when we met Pauline. The smells that wafted into our house from her kitchen was, well, less than appetizing. It didn't happen daily, but often enough that I knew I was forever a meat eater.

The only other downside was Dan. He did not own the farm, but was the grounds keeper and therefore allowed to use it to house his pigs. He was allowed to use the land for free as payment for mowing the grass, tending the house repairs, and collecting rent. Dan was also an alcoholic, and professed often that "beer-thirty" could happen at any point in the day for him. He had a thing for Pauline's daughter too. That was awkward for all of us. Pauline hated it, and Stephanie was not a fan of the arrangement either. Another issue we quickly realized with Dan was that he had a fear of dogs.

If Stephanie's dogs got loose while Dan was there he would have a cussing fit. We tried to steer clear of him. He hated dogs because they were "disease ridden", and he was afraid they were going to affect his hogs. Stomper didn't like Dan either. Anytime Dan came by, Stomper grew the mohawk along his back which told us he was not ok with this man being near his family.

Stomper was quickly becoming a guard dog. We did not really need a guard dog, but he either did not know that or just did not care. His kennel was in our bedroom and when the family got home, Stomper would perform a walk-through of the house before letting us know he needed to go outside. He would sniff the air, walk into every room and even check out the closets if they were available for investigation. His "inspection walk" was like a soldier manning his post, diligent and methodical. Stomper just wanted to protect this family he loved.

The farmhouse had its perks, the biggest of which was free heat. In Maine, we were told by many that we should budget around $3,000-$3,500 for our heating cost each winter. That seemed insane to us, but they were right. Most homes had propane furnaces which had to be filled up monthly. I have had the unpleasant experience of having to carry a fifteen gallon jug of "K1" fuel to the side of the house where the winds ripped through my down-lined coat in 17 degrees below freezing temperatures. We had run out of heat in our house, and the propane company couldn't get to us for a couple of days due to their backlog. This house had the heat bill included in the cost, and I didn't have to do anything with it. It was great, but after another difficult winter Dan came to tell us that rent was going up another $200 to compensate for the uptick in heat. These were familiar words and a familiar situation. It was time to move, again.

Tammy was on the hunt yet again for a good home. She made several calls until she found a house in Auburn. It was closer to my job and our church, but it meant the kids would have to change schools, again. The move happened over summer break, so we hoped the kids would get a fresh start in their new school with little issues. Isaac, Ian and Eli were all in elementary together. The middle school was just a few miles down the road.

That summer Tammy started a new, full-time job working at the call center for the same bank I worked for. We were in different buildings on opposite ends of town, which led to a small problem. The boys lived so close to school that no bus would pick them up. So we had to come up with a solution because neither Tammy nor I got off work early enough to pick the boys up.

Our oldest child Hannah arrived home off the bus early enough to be home for a few minutes before the boys got out of school, so we decided she could walk the three blocks to pick them up. Hannah would walk down the hill, cross the road to the school, then walk the boys back home. Hannah had a phone, so we were able to communicate with her in the event that one of the boys decided he wanted to act up. The plan was great except for one issue. Hannah was scared. Seven years earlier she had been run over on our church campgrounds by a vehicle with a covered trailer loaded to the hilt. The person driving? Me.

Tammy and I had been asked to take care of the Children's Church sessions for our Kentucky district family camp. We directed the Children's Ministry at our home church in Eminence right after we were married, and were both part of ministry teams before we ever met. We had the experience to do this, and were honored to be asked.

We solicited the help of Tammy's niece from Maine, Courtney and six more teens from our church. We also asked Stephen and Stacey Hicks for help that week. They were Children's Ministers at a church in Lexington, KY. Stephen was part of our first puppet team Tammy and I put together in Eminence. They continue to be trusted friends and collaborators on many projects to this day even though we live several hours apart.

Our focus for the week was to teach the kids that their prayers matter to God as much as any adult's prayers do, and even more so when you consider the teachings of Jesus and the child-like faith we should all possess. I often tell kids they have an advantage because adults have to re-learn to be like a child. Children just need to remember not to let their faith change.

It was Friday night and we were dressed for one last service. We would then drive back home late that evening. We had everything loaded in the half-ton trailer and it was busting at the seams. It was filled to the top with puppet gear, the luggage of 7 teenage girls, and the luggage for a family of six. Eli was born not two months before the event and we needed a way to keep his formula cold, so we even packed a portable fridge.

The campground was fenced in which provided a safe place for children to play without the need for a constant watch by parents. Hannah had made several friends that week and had just begun saying bye to them. I could see her about forty yards away when I closed the door to the trailer. I walked to the front of the van and got in to pull up closer to the church. How she got from where she had been to where she ended up so quickly, I'll never know. Courtney was on the side of the road watching my cousin Brandon and I drive the van away. She was terrified at what she saw. My seven-year-old Hannah was riding on the ball hitch of the trailer, and Cortney knew her leg might get caught up in the steel bars when I turned the corner.

Courtney yelled out to her, "Hannah!"

Hannah heard her name, and knowing the tone that was used knew she had made a mistake. Thinking she could position herself to get off before her Dad started driving any faster, she stood to her feet. She was standing on the hitch to jump off when one of her feet slipped. Hannah slid under the trailer and blacked out. She doesn't remember what happened next, which is probably for the best. Courtney was standing on the driver's side of the van, and two Apostolic preacher friends were having a conversation on the opposite side. Rev. Raymond Clark and Rev. Ed Enmen watched as Hannah went under the trailer. From her shoulder the tire caught Hannah's head between it and the road, shattering her glasses. Rev. Clark accounted with tears in his eyes, "The tire dribbled her head on the asphalt like a basketball!"

The first week and a half after the incident, Hannah could cross her legs and you could see the tire tread bruises where the tire rolled up her legs, rolled her over at the waist, and then ran diagonally from her lower left hip to her right shoulder. When she was rolled by the tire, her left arm was punctured by the two bolts that held the wheel in place.

I saw the commotion from my friends and realized something was terribly wrong. I looked in my driver's side mirror just in time to see a small pair of legs, and the bottom of the little yellow dress I had helped her into just an hour earlier. I just knew at that moment, that I had killed my daughter. I flung the van in park and ran to the back of the trailer, not knowing what I would see. My heart had stopped beating and didn't start again until I rounded the corner. Hannah was on her feet and she was yelling out for me!

"Daddy! Daddy, I can't find my glasses!" I was on the verge of panicked, but held it together as best I could. Both sides of her head were covered in blood and gravel and she was bleeding from her left arm, holding it up with her right hand. Her legs were covered in dirt and gravel, and that little yellow dress was ripped to shreds.

"Baby, you can't be walking around. You have to sit down," I said as I forced her to sit back down on the ground.

Several people were witnesses to what happened. There are several cottages on the campground and Rev. Allan Browning (the Kentucky District Secretary for our church organization) was standing at the glass door of his cottage when it happen. He checked on Hannah multiple times while she recovered. His wife later told me that she had never heard him scream like that, and though she hadn't witnessed it, she knew something horrible had just happened.

I sat Hannah down on the pavement, and laid across her legs because she kept trying to get up. There was an EMT who had been there for camp that week. He ran over, crouched down behind her and held her head while I talked to her.

"Baby, we need to pray," I said as calmly as I could. We began to pray and the crowd around us began to grow as we waited for the ambulance to get there. All of a sudden the crowd separated like parting waters and Tammy came running into the scene with reckless abandon.

One of the teenagers present had run into the tabernacle where she was watching our boys and exclaimed, "Tammy, hurry! Craig just ran over Hannah in the parking lot!"

Tammy had her medical background and she instantly surveyed the situation. Her response was simple, "Baby, we need to pray." Although I considered it my fault, but she never once laid the blame on me. I can't begin to explain what a blessing that was during my healing process afterward. The campus nurse arrived and began checking her responses. "Follow my pen, sweetie. Do you know your name? When is your birthday? What day of the week is it?" Hannah responded to everything well, but there was a looming truth that we all noticed. Hannah's head was swelling, and we could all see it.

I was calm on the outside, because Hannah needed me to be. On the inside I was screaming in total terror! When she looked at me with those big blue eyes that were struggling to focus and asked the question, "Daddy, am I going to die?" I was petrified!

Now, we are not parents that lie to our children. Instead of telling our kids about a Santa that comes down your chimney, we opt for the real story of St. Nicholas who made and brought toys to less fortunate children of his village. We have always been honest about things with our children, but I could see blood stains on the shoulders of her yellow dress from her ears, and I was watching her head swell. Honestly, at that moment I was asking myself if this was the moment to say "I love you" one more time, or to say the things you always mean to say but never get around to it. My baby girl has just asked me a question that I didn't have an answer for.

There is a scripture in the Bible that I have always quoted but never fully understood the weight of until that moment. Philippians 4:7 says, "And the peace of God, which passeth all understanding, shall keep your hearts and minds through Christ Jesus." I felt a peace that poured over me, and at that moment, I knew she wasn't going to die.

"No, baby. You aren't going to die. You are going to be ok." I said. In my mind I did not have a definition for what "ok" was, but I knew our daughter was not going to die.

The ambulance arrived and the EMT's immediately called for a helicopter to meet them in a field to fly her to the children's hospital in Louisville. Tammy flew in the helicopter with Hannah, and I made provisions for the boys with family who was there and got in my van to drive to the hospital. I literally had people stand in front of the van telling me I could not drive myself. They kept telling me, "You're in shock."

I replied, "I am not in shock. My daughter needs me strong, and that is exactly what I will be." I drove to the hospital and family members followed me in their van with the boys. The cold reality that was not known to me yet, was that I would be taking anti-depressants for the next eighteen months.

My cousin Scott called me and said, "Hey, Craig. Man, if you have room in there can I ride with you? It's crowded in here with everybody and it'll help us out." I knew that he did not want me driving alone, and honestly I really was ok at the moment, but his company was appreciated.

When the helicopter landed, there was a doctor on the roof waiting. He looked in Hannah's ears and said, "She has bleeding behind both eardrums. Mom, you need to prepare yourself. All signs tell me she has a fractured skull."

When I arrived in the ER they were just finishing Hannah's CAT scan. The technician came out and said, "I'm not sure what the doctor saw on the roof, but there's no sign of any bleeding, or any old blood for that matter." Where had the blood gone, the blood that had ran from Hannah's ears?

Meanwhile, as the dust was settling back at the campgrounds, parents began looking for their own children to hold a little closer. That is what you do in a situation like that. The parents began searching, but momentarily their search came up short. After a few minutes of probing, they finally locate them.

We had taught the kids all week about the power in the prayers of a child. When the situation happened in the parking lot, independent of any leadership, the kids got together and went to the children's chapel to pray for Hannah. She had been covered in blood in the parking lot and the doctor saw bleeding behind the eardrums. But sometime between the doctor's diagnoses and the CAT scan, the blood had completely vanished. No one will ever convince me that God is not real, or that prayer doesn't work. To me, that was concrete proof!

The hospital ran a second CAT scan the next morning to make sure they hadn't missed anything. On the way to the lab, an assistant asked Hannah what happened. I was right behind the assistant to hear the testimony of my seven-year-old daughter.

"My dad ran over me last night with a trailer, but Jesus sent his angels to protect me. And that's why I'm not dead."

Within 48 hours of being ran over by 3/4 of a ton, Hannah walked out of the hospital with injuries equivalent to a bad bike wreck. She had road rash on both sides of her face that healed up in a little over a week, thanks to Tammy's diligence in putting medicated cream on them so often. She had two puncture wounds on her left arm that we now call her "miracle marks". Her only bone affected was the bone just above her growth plate.

Now you understand why Hannah was nervous about walking two blocks, crossing a busy street, getting her brothers and returning the same way. It had been seven years, but the feelings of that awful day were still there. She was hesitant.

"I'm scared," she had told us.

We had exhausted all lead and just did not have an alternative with both of us working.

"Hannah, how can we make it easier for you," we coaxed.

"Can I take Stomper?" Ha! She couldn't even say it without smiling.

Stomper knows his family. He can study how we walk into a room and almost immediately know how to react to our appearance. That intuitiveness was Hannah's strength for the task we were asking her to do.

We made it a point to get acquainted with the crossing guards that assisted the kids after school. These were wonderful people who genuinely cared about the kids, and we came to know them well. They also loved Stomper, and he loved them. He was so careful to keep Hannah in mind while walking. If she slowed her pace, Stomper would stop looking around and focus on her. He'd nudge close to her to reassure her that he was there. He even looked both ways before crossing the road to keep her safe.

"I have a guard dog!" Hannah said with excitement. The only times he didn't walk with her to get her brothers was in the dead of winter because we were worried about his paws getting frost bite. We tried booties, once.

At the time of this story it has been nine years since Hannah's accident, and it still affects me. Hannah has conquered her anxiety, but I still make the kids line up like ducklings with Tammy in the front, then oldest to youngest until we get across whatever parking lot we're trying to navigate. It has gotten better, and we can even talk about it openly, but it still troubles me. Hannah loves taking Stomper for walks. He growls a bit at teenagers riding their bikes too close to her and will even let out a quiet "woof" to make his presence known.

Our amazing boxer who had just a year prior been afraid to walk up and down stairs because of fear, was now helping our teenager conquer her own fear. It was the love for his family that caused this to happen. Being responsive to the needs of Hannah in those moments of insecurity, Stomper was showing maturity and responsibility in his bond of love. We learned in that time that we should all work to apply those characteristics to our own bonds, showing ripeness in our fruit of love.

6 CHAPTER NAME

We learned a lot on that first day of school. Hannah was so excited, and full of confidence after just one day. She told her story:

**"I was really nervous at first, but Stomper was so excited about walking that it made it ok. When we got to the first crossing guard he started growling, like a long way away from her. He kept leaning against me like he wanted me to stay away, but as we got closer he started**

to calm down. Miss Carla is sweet and wouldn't harm a fly. I guess Stomper just figured it out.

She asked if she could pet him. I looked at his back and he didn't have a mohawk, so I said it was ok. She walked right up to him. Stomper nudged her leg with his head to say 'hi'. She helped us across the street to the next crossing guard. It's like Stomper knew these people were here to help.

We made it to the school with no problems. I waited on the side of the school for the boys with the other pickup people. When the kids started coming out, Stomper started breathing faster. He loves kids. Several of them came up to pet him. He loved it.

The walk home was great. The first crossing guard on the way back motioned for us to cross, and as Stomper passed him he let out a grunt like he was saying 'thank you'. That's what the crossing guard thought too.

He looked at Stomper and said, 'Your welcome.'

Ian piped in and said, 'He's deaf. He can't hear you.' The crossing guard was shocked. I don't know why but he thought that was amazing.

Stomper was like a celebrity around the school. People kept asking if he was really deaf while we walked home. Some of the smaller kids wanted to learn the signs so they could tell him to do something.

When they would do the sign for 'sit' and Stomper responded they would jump up and down, 'Mommy, mommy! I know sign language!' It was amazing!"

Stomper was officially the family guardian. We did not expect him to, but he loved us so much that he volunteered for the job. Hannah's fear was gone and she was back to her confident self. She is still cautious to this day around vehicles but she isn't afraid anymore, and Stomper helped her with that. He made sure she made it to school and back to the house safely every day.

As time went on we had to follow a specific method of introduction with Stomper that we have continued to use with each new visitor that Stomper meets. The checklist is constructed as follows:

- The visitor is warned before their arrival that their first few minutes of the meet-and-greet is about Stomper meeting the visitor, and NOT the visitor meeting Stomper. That will come later.
- Stomper considers me as the alpha of the family, so as he sees me talking to the visitor he will settle down.
- The leash is ALWAYS on during the introduction time. It will be removed when he stops growling, and his body settles down.
- You may pet him when he nudges your hand. Congratulations, you are officially approved!

This list came about through some trial and error. We had family that would come over and cause Stomper to bark, but he had no issues with them because he had known them since his adoption. It was made very clear that he would bark and growl, and this was not cause to be alarmed.

Stomper uses his voice, often I might add. He uses it to warn other animals to get out of his yard, he grumbles when he's frustrated, and if something peaks his interest he will let out a little "woof". He even tries to scare the light reflection on the ceiling when we fill his water bowl up in the sink and carry it to his eating area. That light isn't supposed to be there, and Stomper wants to make sure the light knows that!

Because of his deafness he has no idea how loud he can be. Those of us who can hear, naturally learn this from hearing others. Hopefully, kids learn not to yell indoors at an early age. "Use your inside voice" we tell them. It is learned behavior. But when you are deaf, how are you supposed to know the difference between soft levels and loud levels?

Stomper is loud, and it is a different kind of bark from most I have heard. It travels from his gut to his throat. It is a deep and boisterous bark, yet remains in his throat. My cousin, Doug, would complain that even prolonged laughter would hurt his throat. He couldn't hear how other people used their voice, and did not have an understanding of voice placement. With Stomper, all of these factors became a part of our lives. We had to figure things out in the beginning, but then it became second nature. Life with our boxer seemed to us as normal. It was a normal that many could not fully grasp or appreciate.

We were in that house for a year, and God opened a door that we were not expecting. Indiana.

We lived in Maine for a little more than two years. We loved our time there, and made lasting friendships and memories with our family. One thing I have learned is that God does not always reveal His full plans. I often say that there is a reason why God shows you the promise before you see the road to get there. Usually it's because the road doesn't make sense. We were in that beautiful farmhouse with all the land for a year, then God opened a door to another move. We were heading to the crossroads of America.

It was difficult leaving Kentucky because of our church. We had a strong relationship with our Pastoral family, but had felt a disconnect from our church. We loved the people we worshipped with, and struggled to understand why we were having such a difficult time feeling as though we were a part of the congregation. We didn't realize God was working in that time to prepare our hearts for a new chapter. After living in Maine for two years we found ourselves in the same boat, and unsure why God had plans for history to repeat itself. Pastor Maroney, our Pastor from Kentucky, had been voted in as Pastor at Abundant Faith Church in Evansville, Indiana in the fall of 2014. When we heard the news Tammy and I both knew this was why we were feeling the disconnect in Maine. We had never been to Evansville before, but there was a definite draw toward a new adventure.

Tammy and I spent a considerable amount of time praying and fasting about it before coming to the same conclusion. We were moving to Evansville, Indiana. The

Maroney's urged us to visit first to get a feel for the church and city. However, with our jobs that was an impossibility. We just knew by prayer and fasting that this was right choice and God was in it.

We had a great relationship with our Associate Pastor (now Pastor), Reverend Todd Little, of the First United Pentecostal Church of Lewiston, and his family in Maine. I approached him with the news about our feeling the call to leave, and how I had a job lined up and housing secured in a short amount of time.

"I don't want to hear about jobs and housing falling into place," he quickly said. "Is it the Will of God?"

"Yes," was my confident reply.

"Then that's all I need to hear." I love him even though he still playfully refers to me as a 'cockroach' for leaving… at least I think it's playful.

We loaded our SUV, rented a trailer and headed toward the Indiana boarder. There was a small community just outside of Evansville that we decided to call home. It was a family neighborhood with a lot of kids and they all played in the streets together. There was one family that seemed to be at the heart of everything going on, and of course they lived right beside us.

Our property had the only paved driveway in the area with kids living in the house. We so happened to have a basketball goal and everyone wanted to be at our house. This was a culture shock and the polar opposite of our Maine experience. In Maine we had neighbors that welcomed us to the neighborhood on our arrival, and did not speak to us again until we were loading up to leave. They were always friendly, but just not sociable. We hung out with family and a few friends in Maine, but all of that was done at scheduled times in scheduled places. Stomper had helped us solidify a schedule that just worked, but now all of that was being disrupted.

The reason we loved this house was because of the big back yard. The house sat on the front half of a full acre lot. We had two trees in the front yard and that was all. The back yard had a shed for storage and was fully fenced in. Stomper no longer needed a leash to go outside and it was a great setup. The gate leading to the driveway was made of chain-link fencing, and there was privacy fencing on the right side and in the back. On the opposite side of the yard was more chain-link fencing that connected to the other side of the house, making the back yard half chain-link and half privacy fencing.

The first time Tammy and I showed the house to our kids, we took Stomper outside to show him his new play area. He looked worried that we didn't have his leash on him but darted toward the edges of the yard to sniff around and mark a few spots. Then he saw the area where the chain-link portion was connected to the house. In the darkness the chain-link was not visible and it looked like an open area. Stomper froze when he noticed it. He looked at us, then back at the fence.

"Oh, no... He thinks it's open," I said as I watched him consider his next action.

He took a step back and lunged forward toward what he thought was absolute freedom. We all screamed at him, but it was useless. With head down and running full throttle, the entire family watched helplessly as he collided with the invisible chain-link fencing. His head pushed and swelled the fence out toward the road, and then as it retracted it catapulted Stomper like a slingshot back towards us knocking him to the ground. He shook his head trying to make the stars go away, and finally came to his senses. Standing up at last, Stomper walked over to us and just sat down. He sure got a lot of love from us for that painful lesson.

The revelation in that moment was that the leash wasn't holding him back from freedom, but it was there for his protection. He realized his humans seemed to know things he didn't know. The leash has been our only means of communication at times when Stomper is focused in on something. Two tugs means he needs to look at whomever is holding the other end of the leash because we need to tell him something. This is a principle our kids learned many years earlier.

When the kids were younger we would fly kites. We had access to a big field in Kentucky that could facilitate four kites flying without the worry of tangling lines and crying kids. The message was the same every time: Don't let go of the string.

One windy fall afternoon we were flying our kites. It was an interesting time because there was a wind stream about forty feet in the air and if you wanted the kite to go higher, there was a patch of sky above that wind stream that was nearly motionless. The kids were having a difficult time getting the hang of bringing the kite above  that spot, and admittedly it took me a few tries as well.

The key to rising above the empty space was to create wind for the kite yourself. We learned through some trial and error where the threshold was, and when we hit that ceiling it was time to move our feet. If you ran with the kite when the wind was dead you could still keep the kite in the air because of resistance created at the other end of the tether. As I ran to keep the kite afloat, I kept tension on the string and began lengthening it at the same time to cause the kite to rise. Once the kite rose another fifteen feet or so, there was another pocket of air that picked up on the fun. From these heights the kids were able to release almost all of the string on their spool. Those kites flew so high that people told us later that they could see them from more than a half mile into town. We got some great pictures that day.

Hannah was twelve years old at the time. She was frustrated with the process, but once she got her kite high enough she moved back to her original position and enjoyed the flight. Isaac was nine, and he grasped the concept the fastest. He loves to run and it was easy for him to run all over the field to get the kite high enough. Elijah was four, so in order for him to accomplish it Tammy had to help. Ian was seven at the time and very adventurous. He loved the learning aspect of what we were doing, and being above average academically with a scientist's mind, he was always up for a little experimentation.

"Dad, what would happen if I let go?"

"Well, if you let go it will fly for a while, and if it goes too high you'll lose the kite."

"Why?"

"Because, Ian, you are the anchor. Without an anchor it will go wherever the wind takes it."

"Oh," he concluded, and that was the end of that. I walked away.

I do not know if he wasn't paying attention or experimenting to see if Dad was telling the truth, but a short moment later we heard a cry for help. I turned to see a yellow handle floating in the air and quickly sprinted toward the tree line at the end of the field to catch it. I guess the kids just weren't used to seeing ole' Dad run, because the laughter that echoed in that field would have made most standup comedians jealous. I did catch the handle though. Once anchored back to the ground the kite stopped thrashing wildly and continued its normal flight pattern.

I thought Ian had learned his lesson, but then it happened again. Isaac's kite was on the ground, so Isaac ran after it this time and caught it. The third time we were not so lucky.

The kite had risen to a height that we couldn't reach and we watched as that yellow handle flew up into the trees. It soon got tangled in the branches, but the kite was flying high above the tree line. It had found a new wind pocket which kept it flying out of reach until after dark. The kite had done what it was designed to do, fly. The string had done what it was designed to do, tether. But the anchor didn't hold so the kite had found a new anchor.

I have used this story over the years to remind my kids that if their mother Tammy and I stop being parents so that we can be buddies, they will only find something else to anchor to. This might cause them to go places and do things that are too dangerous. The tethers aren't too restrict, but have always been to protect and hold it all together.

After Stomper slammed his head into the fence he learned his lesson, and never ran full speed into the fence again. The four fencing walls were his boundaries. They kept him safe from cars he couldn't hear, and neighborhood kids who didn't know how to treat animals. Unfortunately, the family of five who lived next door was causing a few problems.

The family had lived there for more than six years and their three boys felt like they ruled the neighborhood. The boys rode their bikes up and down the streets with reckless abandon. They would come onto our driveway to shoot basketball on our goal, and hit our van with their bikes as they rode around. We had to tell them daily not to ride in our grass or around our vehicle.

"This is not your yard. You need to stop coming over here," we had explained.

"Well, the last guy that lived here let us come over and play." We happened to know the last guy lived there with his elderly mother and probably got tired of telling them to go home.

"Well that guy doesn't live here anymore, and we don't want you scuffing up our van, or getting hurt on our property."

"You're mean!" they would retort, then go play in the street. They were certainly not fans of Stomper either. We would find Nerf darts in our yard that they'd shoot over the fence to try and hit Stomper. At first we gave them back, then we noticed he wasn't a fan of them. Tammy would stand in the kitchen and watch them throw balls and sticks to try and hit him. I even picked up a dirty diaper once. She would step outside to tell them to stop, but they never listened.

I even went to their parents to try and reason with them on several occasions, but quickly realized where the kids got their mean little attitudes from. This couple was more worried about our "pit bull" getting out and hurting one of their kids than trying to deal with their kids antagonizing our BOXER. They were unconcerned with their boys throwing things over the fence and just wanted to talk about Stomper barking so much.

"He doesn't realize he's barking so loud. If you'll look at him you'll see he's actually more excited to see people than trying to attack them. You have to keep in mind that this is now his yard, and he feels he needs to protect it," I tried to explain.

One day Tammy was getting on those boys for climbing onto the back of the fence and getting Stomper wound up. The dad came out the back door yelling at her, because she was getting on to their kids in their yard. Their intention was to challenge Stomper and get him worked up. He was barking, but since they were technically on their property the dad didn't seem to find a problem with the scenario. "I'll promise you this," the dad yelled across the fence, "If he comes in my yard I'm gonna shoot him!"

Shoot him? Why would anyone see that as an option? I was confident Stomper wasn't interested in harming anyone but they just couldn't see it that way.

Our oldest three kids rode the bus to school and back. Eli couldn't because the elementary school we wanted him in didn't have a bus that came into our area. Tammy had picked me up from work and Eli up from school, and we were on our way home when her phone rang. Hannah called us when she walked in the door every day to let us know that she and the boys were home. It was like clockwork. If she called after that we knew someone must be up.

"Yes, Hannah?" Tammy answered with a parental anticipation as she put Hannah on speaker phone.

"Uh, Mom. There is a cop car in our driveway, and the cop is knocking on the door. We're scared!"

"A cop?" I said from the passenger's side.

"Yes sir. I have the boys in your bedroom with Stomper, and we are watching him....Okay, he's leaving. What does he want?"

"Well, how are we supposed to know?" I said in a sort of worried disgust.

"Hannah, you guys stay in the room. We'll be home in a couple of minutes, and we'll call the police department to see what's going on."

Tammy had a tone in her voice that calmed the situation. As we turned into our subdivision we passed the police officer. We pulled into the driveway and there were our pesky neighbors. Mason, the youngest walked right up to me as I got out of the van and proclaimed, "My mom called the cops on your dog. He was barking at us."

"Mason! Get over here." His mom said as she scurried into their house.

Sure enough, the officer came back to our house ten minutes later. We sent the kids to their rooms with Stomper, who could sense there was something going on. I opened the door, and a tall officer in his early twenties was standing there ready to have a conversation about our dog. We invited him in.

After talking for a few minutes and explaining the whole story to him, he was extremely understanding. "Stomper only roams in our fenced in back yard. If he's in the front at all he's on his leash." Tammy told him.

We went on to share that the real issue was the neighbor boys climbing on the fence and getting Stomper worked up. "If they would just stay out of our yard, Stomper would have no issues with them," we told him.

"I understand. Pits are territorial dogs," the officer started to say.

"Pit? He's a boxer!" I chimed in.

"Oh, they said he was a pit." He continued. "Still, boxers want to protect their homes too."

"Exactly." We continued the conversation for a bit, then he left to talk more with the neighbors about keeping the kids in their own yard. They didn't stop.

The neighboring dad got a job in Kentucky, and the family moved after a year of us dealing with their antics. Stomper never got out of the yard, and those kids never stayed in theirs.

Doctor Stephen R Covey once said, "Seek first to understand, then to be understood." We use moments like these to teach our kids that, assuming you know a thing, is not as accurate as asking questions for a true understanding. We all make opinions about a situation based on our current understanding. Any news you see says pit bulls are dangerous and that they attack people. If we understood the conditions those dogs were subjected to, or consider that they are placed in an environment that is 'kill or be killed', then we might understand the reasoning behind an alleged attack. Any animal would be subject to act out if treated cruelly, as would many humans. But Stomper is a white boxer, and we have had that conversation so many times. Still, people's truths are based solely on their current knowledge.

What would happen if we sought understanding before judgment? I believe we could make our little corner of the world better along the relationships we facilitate within that world.

## CHAPTER 7 - RELATIONSHIPS

Now that we were in Indiana, my family was only a few hours away. My mother couldn't have been happier! She had flown for the first time when she visited us in Maine. She learned to navigate the airports just fine and enjoyed her time there, but make no mistake, she was thrilled about being able to drive the two hour trek to Indiana. Stomper's facial recognition has been something I have always admired about him. I have had several dogs in my life, but I have never had one, or known of one as intuitive as Stomper. Stomper knew it was my mom every time. His excitement level kicked up a notch. Why? Because Mawmaw brought treats!

Stomper makes it clear that his first priority in life is his family, but he can easily be persuaded by food and snacks. He was definitely born to be a part of this family! When Mom came in the house he would nudge her to say 'hello', then sniff out his treat.

Stomper has a different relationship for all six of the family members in our house. I had to teach him not to jump up on people because his enthusiasm could be painful. With me, he bounces on his front paws and occasionally jumps a bit but not too much because it hurts his hip and leg. Then he will walk to my feet and sit down to wait for me to greet him. I can look at him without moving for the longest time, and he will not budge. I not sure he even breathes. Once I greet him, he will continue his bouncing with the same level of excitement. Daddy's home.

Tammy receives a different greeting. Stomper is always excited to see her, but does not jump on her. He walks to her and nudges her a bit. She typically has her arms full of groceries, bags or other things, so Stomper knows to keep his distance until she puts them down. Tammy is also the only one in the family that Stomper uses his voice to communicate with on a regular basis through groans and short barks. She knows whether he needs to be let out, or is out of fresh water. I'll emphasize fresh! If Stomper gets some food in his water bowl, which happens often, the water bowl must be filled with fresh water. And he growls at the light reflection all the way back to his bowl.

The kids each have their own relationship with Stomper too. Hannah likes to walk around the neighborhood, and almost always takes Stomper with her. He grumbles if she doesn't take him. When she puts her sneakers on, Stomper, he just knows he's going walking! To see him prancing up and down the road is always heartwarming. I often wonder if he is remembering the times he walked Hannah to school, and the change in her that he helped build. Hannah loves her newfound freedom and confidence that Stomper has instilled in her.

To make Stomper's bed, Tammy and I used a four inch thick piece of foam and cut it into a rectangle using an electric meat cutter, then bought material to cover it. You'll find it in the living room against a wall usually, but that DIY bed makes road trips with us now as well. That is Stomper's spot until Isaac gets involved. He'll pull the bed out, and sit on it with Stomper on his lap. They are great friends. Isaac has more energy than the rest of the family combined! He is the first to run and play fetch in the back yard with Stomper. Even in the evenings when we are chilling in the living room, Isaac won't sit on the couch. He wants to hang out with Stomper on his dog bed.

Ian is an inside kid. He'll go ride his bike or jump on the trampoline, but he loves to draw and has an artist's heart. He has the biggest imagination of any twelve-year old I have ever known. If the other kids are playing ball or doing something else outside, you may find Ian at the table or on the couch drawing his latest art piece. If Stomper can't be outdoor with anyone else, he'll make his way to Ian's feet and lay down in front of him. Stomper loves people for the most part, but most of all he just wants to be close to his family.

Eli is a well-rounded kid. He is happy inside or outside and that works out great for our boxer. Stomper loves playing chase with him in the back yard. Base is always the trampoline where Eli can leap on so that Stomper doesn't catch him. Eli is great at tug of war too!

When we eat our family supper we eat at the table, and the kitchen table is a place of conversation. We find out what happened at school while we were at work. We talk about our jobs and everything that happens away from home

Tammy and I know who our kids are crushing on, and we are always helping if they are struggling with something. Our teens act like your typical teens, but we pull it out of them... most of the time. At supper time, Stomper has a spot at the table too. His spot is under the table. He knows we may be there for a while so he lays down and dog-naps. As a deaf dog, there were times early on that we would leave the table and Stomper would just continue sleeping. He finally learned that if he was touching someone when they got up, their movement would wake him up and he could move from the table with us. Now whenever we eat, he has a paw on someone's foot before he drifts off into his slumbering sleep.

Indiana was a great move, and it has been confirmed to us many times over that we made the right decision. We became close to a lot of friends that we are blessed to have. Our church has an incredible group of people who have blessed our lives so much. I love that you also never know who may pay a visit. One Sunday morning a young lady in her early twenties came in as a guest. She was of Asian descent, but seemed quite snobby. Several people including myself, introduced themselves and shook her hand to welcome her to our service. She shook our hands and refused to say anything. A few members of our church believed she might not understand English.

We were preparing for a baptism at the end of service when our Pastor's wife went to introduce herself to the young lady. She asked her a few questions with no response, when finally the girl pointed to her ears indicating that she was deaf. Sister Maroney knows a little sign language, but no more than the basics. She told the lady to hold on for a minute while she signaled for me to come over and talk to her. I introduced myself to her with a burst of excitement. She had made a friend with a police officer who attends our church. He had invited her to come but was working that day, so she knew none of us there. For the sake of her privacy I will refer to her as Lacy.

Tammy invited her to go eat with us. She didn't want to, but we finally convinced her. It was the quietest meal we've ever had as I interpreted Lacy's conversation for the family, and then their words back to her. I was shocked at how much American Sign Language I had retained. It had been eight years since I had conversed in ASL, other than communicating with Stomper.

Young Lacy had an incredible story. As she told it, she was born to Chinese parents, but in the country of Kazakhstan. Not one person bothered to speak or communicate with her for the first eight years of Lacy's life. Finally, an American family adopted her, and brought her to the United States. Her new mother taught her sign language so that she was able to communicate, but something happened between the family and Lacy. I was never clear what that was, but Lacy was sent into the foster care system. She was then adopted by a family who only took in older kids for a few years, then turned them out on their own when they turned eighteen. The family could no longer receive a check for the kids, so they were on their own with nothing to their name.

So you can understand when I say Lacy had some attachment issues. In spite of it all, she gravitated to my family. The kids fell in love with her, and Tammy was constantly texting her to make sure she had everything she needed. Tammy took her groceries, and we had taken her out to eat several times. We decided we wanted to have her over for supper.

"My dog understands sign language," I told her. Lacy was shocked!

"No way. I don't believe you."

"It's true. You'll meet him when you come over."

So the date was set, much to the excitement of everyone! We had rehearsed our introduction routine and we were all set. The leash was on Stomper as the door opened and Lacy walked in. What happened next, I'll never understand. The entire family spun around to look as Stomper reacted to the new visitor. Stomper let out a guttural howl with his mouth almost fully closed. It was subdued, yet full of excitement at the same time. He saw Lacy and immediately sat down beside me. My mouth literally dropped. I looked at Tammy for an explanation as to what was going on. The kids were shocked as well. What was he doing? He had never acted this way.

"I'm going to let him go," I said confidentially.

"Craig, are you sure?" Tammy responded, but I had already taken the leash off. Stomper stood up and calmly walked toward Lacy. "Craig," Tammy said nervously.

Stomper sat in front of Lacy and began wagging his little nub tail. Lacy began speaking to him using ASL, and Stomper responded! In disbelieve, Lacy squealed with excitement. She sat on the couch as we all stepped back to watch in amazement, mesmerized that a bond had formed between Stomper and Lacy so quickly. Lacy told Stomper to sit, and Stomper sat. Lacy could only laugh. She asked for his paw, and Stomper responded. She laughed even more, and I would have joined except I began to have another one of those allergy attacks. As I began wiping the tears from my eyes, Lacy told him to lay down. Can you believe that Stomper responded better to her than he does anyone; even me? Could Stomper possibly know that she was deaf like him? As we had supper that evening, Stomper never left her side. Lacy came over to our house several times over the next few weeks, and even spent the night a couple of times. Stomper was equally excited every single time.

It was near Thanksgiving and my family decided they would come to our house to celebrate. Tammy and I usually cooked and prepped the majority of the meals for the big holidays, so it only made sense. Tammy was concerned about where Lacy was going and it seemed she had no plans. "You will have Thanksgiving with us then." Tammy insisted.

The plans were set, so we spent most of the day prepping for our company. The garage was set up for the tables, so we decorated them and cooked while the kids cleaned and helped in the kitchen. We had seven visitors not counting my aunt's dog. He was a rescue dog and she loved him dearly. This was the first time we had another dog in our house since our neighbor's pit bull puppy ran into our upstairs home in Maine.

Stomper and his new friend loved one another from the start. They played and ran around the back yard until they were both worn out. With the festivities over, my family headed back to Kentucky that evening and Lacy stayed for the night. It was beginning to feel like we had a fifth child. Stomper loved her, the kids loved her, and Tammy and I were growing very fond of her. We started planning for Christmas the following week.

Tammy found out that Lacy didn't have a tree in her apartment. She didn't even have a couch, but she was making it somehow. We bought her a small tree that she was so proud of. We were talking about what we were going to get her for Christmas one evening as the kids lay in bed. Tammy had Facebook open, and suddenly blurted out, "No way!"

"What?" I asked.

She just handed her phone to me in silence. My heart literally sank. "Eli is going to be heartbroken." I said. Eli was very close to Lacy, but Lacy had proclaimed on Facebook that she was leaving Indiana and moving out of state to continue her education. We both started texting her.

With her attachment issues, Lacy could not allow herself to get too close to anyone for fear of them betraying her like she had experienced most of her life. As a result, she had decided to leave us first. The conversation with the kids was tear filled and ended in a lot of hugging with unanswered questions from our kids' perspectives. I ended the conversation that night with this statement:

"Guys, you are going to have a lot of people come and go in your life. Some will be permanent and others temporary. It is not our job to determine who fits in which category, but to be blessings to everyone we have the privilege of getting to know. I wish I could guarantee that the heartache you feel right now will never happen again, but that would be a lie. What I can tell you is, each time you give of yourself you become a better person. Always be the better person."

We gave Lacy a nice sendoff with Christmas presents and plenty of hugs. I don't know if we will ever have the opportunity to be that big of a light in someone else's life again, but I know that we gave it everything we had for Lacy.

M. K. Clinton, author of The Returns said, "The world would be a nicer place if everyone had the ability to love as unconditionally as a dog." Dogs love just like that. If you don't treat them great, they will most likely love you anyway. But if you love them the way they want to love you, the reward is a great return on your investment. Stomper has an incredible amount of love for his family, but still has an abundance of it to share with others. I can only hope that as I grow older, I will be able to love people with a Stomper-kind of love. It's complete for the individual. It is specific to the recipient, with an understanding of boundaries.

If only I can learn to love like Stomper.

## CHAPTER 8 - FAMILY

Stomper loves riding in the car. It's a good thing too, because we take several mini road trips throughout the year. We have traveled to Kentucky to see my family for birthday celebrations and other events many times since living in southern Indiana. Because it is a two and a half hour drive, Stomper goes with us. He will move from the floor to his own seat in the back, and then usually ends up resting his head on the kids' laps in the middle section to look out the windows. He has always been content to ride, even for long distances.

In the Hedges' household, family is everything. Tammy and I have said for years that we became parents to be parents, not to put a teenager on the payroll. When we go out to eat, our kids come also. When we go to a friend's house, our kids come also. We have unfortunately drifted apart from friends over this very idea, the ideal that family should be more united than divided. We make strong efforts to create memories together and any time we can work it out, Stomper is along for the journey.

In 2016 we planned a family trip to the Great Smoky Mountains National Park in Tennessee. Hannah, who was now fifteen, was in a stroller the last time we had visited, so none of our other kids had been before. The last time we had visited was for an anniversary celebration early in our marriage. Some of my family, including my mom and brother were also along for the trip. My brother hadn't vacationed there in a long time, and as for my mom, she hadn't been since I was eight years old. So much had changed and built up. We were shocked to see how many newer attractions were mingled in with the old staples as well. We couldn't wait to see our kids' expressions when we got there. Everyone was ecstatic about the trip. We had to make sure we had a place big enough for a family of eleven that would also accommodate our dogs. Tammy searched and found a beautiful secluded cabin deep in the mountains big enough for our family of six, my brother's family of four, and our mom.

We loaded up the van and headed out for the six and a half hour trip to the Smokies. It seems I love a good road trip more than anyone else, so I was elated to be going to a place with gorgeous views and plenty of places to create memories. Although there were several activities that were dog friendly, most of the time we arranged our activities so that we weren't away from the cabin for longer than three to five hours. We did this to make Stomper feel right at home. We had a blast doing what we wanted in Pigeon Forge and Gatlinburg, but spent a lot of time in our cabin. It rained several days, so it was nice to have a place to hang out. Stomper loved the rain, and that meant more family time for him!

We have learned a little something about Stomper during our road trips. First, we've learned that because Stomper is deaf, he doesn't always communicate in a way that people and other animals understand. He often growls while wagging his nub tail, but no one ever looks at the body language of our stocky, one-hundred pound dog. They just hear his growl and back off.

"Yep, those pits are loyal to their family." We will hear them say.

"He's not a pit, he's a boxer."

Stomper is protective of his family for sure, but not so overly protective that he can't socialize with others. We've learned that when he growls, people and animals will get scared. When they get scared, Stomper will sense their fear and get more agitated, but it is their reactions to his growl that spawn the whole situation of miscommunication. So when we were on our trip, Stomper stayed in the cabin, mostly because of this misunderstanding between himself and people who didn't understand him.

The second thing we realized, was that Stomper doesn't care about accommodations. He doesn't care if he has to sleep on a couch or the floor. It doesn't matter where he is as long as he is with his family. What a great lesson to be learned from our dog! We spend so much time constructing life together that often we can't see the beauty of what we are building. There are so many frustrating moments in life that prevents us from seeing the bigger picture. Stomper's laser like focus toward being with his family, is such a great reminder to us about the things that really matter.

Six and a half hours of travel in a van is not an easy thing to do, especially with kids and a dog. By only the third hour in, the kids started to question us about our arrival time. When we got to our cabin in the mountains, Stomper was down for a couple days. He found places on the floor that he could spread out because his hip had been aggravated. We brought meds and administered them to him, but it just wasn't enough for the inflammation and pain that he was dealing with. It took a couple days before he was back to his normal self, and although he still favored the injured hip, he was more mobile.

When we got home it was the very same story. A long road trip was just not worth the pain that he had to go through to take it. Although our trip to the Smokies was a great success, it would be Stomper's last long road trip. There were to be no more trips to Maine, and his trips to Kentucky became very limited as well.

The following summer we made the long trek to Maine to visit Tammy's family. We made arrangements for Stomper to stay with my mom in Kentucky while we were away. It was difficult because we had never left him for very long while on a vacation like this. He had stayed at my mom's house before, but only for a day or two while my family was performing some children's ministry duties at a nearby church. Our entire family was saddened by it, but we knew it was the best decision. The drive to Kentucky to meet my mother proved early on we made the right call.

We had decided to meet my mom at a predetermined exit off Interstate 64 (this interstate runs right through the heart of Kentucky) to hand Stomper over. We were only forty-five minutes from our house on I64 headed towards Louisville when a very unfamiliar, but recognizable sound came from the middle of our van. It was definitely a scream, but it wasn't coming from one of our kids! Driving at nearly 80 mph down the interstate, Tammy and I both simultaneously jerked our heads around to see what had made the ghastly cry. We instantly noticed that Stomp's ears were straight back against his head, and his eyes were full of fear and pain. Something was terribly wrong.

We first thought that Ian had leaned his seat back on Stomper's leg and it was caught, but Ian had not moved. I abruptly pulled into the emergency lane to try figure the situation out. It turns out that Stomper's leg had cramped up on him. The muscle in his hip had constricted so tightly that he could no longer bear it. Tammy quickly put his leash on and coaxed him out onto the side of the road. She walked him back and forth until he began putting his weight back or his cramped hind leg. We knew we had to rearrange some things before we could continue our journey.

The stow-and-go space in the van was stuffed with luggage and overnight bags for our hotel stay and all of it had to come out. One of the seats on the passenger's side was laid into the new empty space on the floor, so the boys were forced to sit three-wide in the back row until we met Mom. We had brought Stomper's bed with us as well, so we laid it out in the open area to give him somewhere comfortable to sit or lay. The only issue with this new arrangement was that we now had to listen to the boys sitting cramped up in the back row grumble from time to time. That moment with Stomper on the way to Kentucky changed everything. Our family trips would look a lot different from here on out.

Mom met us just off the predetermined exit, and after a belabored goodbye we were on our way. We talked often on our trip about how empty it felt without Stomper along for our visit. In Maine, it seems people take their dogs everywhere with them. I've never been anywhere where I've seen so many people out and about with their fur babies. Although we were certain we made the right choice by leaving him with mom, we missed him terribly.

The first few days after we left for Maine we checked on Stomp, and the answer was always the same. "He's fine. He's so precious, but he's not eating. He misses you." It made us sad to think that he wasn't eating because he missed his family. It made things even worse to see so many people with their dogs out and about in Maine. It seemed there was a furry face in every other car we passed, on every sidewalk and even in busy shopping towns like Freeport. There were big dogs and little dogs walking through the crowds with their families. It became all too common that week to hear, "Awe," coming from one of the kids, or even Tammy and I. We missed our boy very bad.

After what seemed like an eternity, the time came for us to make the trek home. We used to drive the eighteen and a half hour trip in one day, so we would get up in the morning and be on the road by 5:00am and drive until 11:30pm. Tammy still has trouble with her back and hip, so this time we split the trip up a bit. After an overnight stay in Pennsylvania, we were finally on our way to see our Stomper!

The meeting place was in a place called LaGrange, KY. There was a Cracker Barrel there, and it seemed like the perfect place to meet. As my brother Clint pulled up to the parking lot, my heart began beating faster. There's jus' something about a family being reunited with a loved one after time apart that causes that. I still have that feeling when I see my wife after a long day's work.

I crouched down low on the lawn as my brother took Stomper out of his vehicle. Stomper took one look at me and let out a loud "Woof!" That bark spoke volumes to me about how Stomper's week had gone. In that solitary bark I heard, "How could you? Why did you leave me? Where did you go? What took you so long? Don't ever do that again! I missed you!"

After Stomper said all that in one bark, he ran to me and buried his head into my body, nearly knocking me over as he pressed his head into my chest. It seemed as if he couldn't get close enough. After we enjoyed our reunion for a couple of minutes, it was time for one of Stomper's favorite games; Leash Obstacle Course!

Leash Obstacle Course is played like this: Stomper walks excitedly through a small crowd of people (our family when we get together), and whoever is on the other end of the leash has to keep up with him. Stomper begins to weave in and out of the crowd to whomever he chooses to show attention to. Keep in mind that he may decide to circle back to the same person any number of times. As the attention order changes depending on where Stomp leads, the leash walker's job is to try to keep themselves from getting tangled up with others in the group. Sometimes the leash walker wins, other times everyone involved loses.

We arrived at home in Indiana that evening around 7:30pm. The trip back was nearly a mirror image of the ride to Kentucky. We put the boys in the back for the ride home and heard a replay of their discontent. Almost immediately upon our arrival back home, Stomper fell back into his routine. He was home! He was with his family.

Distance cannot change the fact that kinfolk are family, and neither good times nor bad times should take anything away from our relationships. I have severed ties with many people over the years because I was certain I was better off without them. Maybe there was some truth to that, but what if I was supposed to help them be a better person? What if the relationship was about me giving to them, instead of receiving from them?

Stomper was angry at me for leaving him to go on our trip. For him it probably felt like ten years instead of ten days, but when we met again he had said his peace. That's when he hugged me. Is it strange to think that he would make a better person than me? I often struggle to let people back into my life that have hurt me. I close chapters in my life, never to return. I rectify those actions by saying to myself, "I don't need them." But what if they need me?

Stomper immediately resumed his role as the white centurion of our house. He checks the rooms to make sure no one is there, he watches out the window to ensure no one tries anything while we are away, and when the kids are outside he wants to be with them to protect them. He'll even lie in the middle of the floor to get a better vantage point of the house at the expense of accidentally getting stepped on by someone who has their own agenda and destination, someone who has forgotten about Stomper being in the floor. His immediate reaction is not to yell or begrudge, but he has a special look in his eye that says, "I apologize for being in your way." To top it off, he will then get up with his bad hip to check on YOU to make sure YOU are alright. Why is it so hard for us as people, to do that for each other?

Stomper is exceptional! His dedication to the six individuals that live and share the same house with him has made us a better family. We are a better team because Stomper has helped us to see the power of love, and taught us that forgiveness and devotion can get us through the toughest of times.

Aristotle once said, "The whole is greater than the sum of its parts." We are all greater together. Stomper has been that reminder for our family. "We will get through this. We're the Hedges." This quote has rung through our house often over the years, and it's the stand that we take to let all who listen know we are in this together; we will win this together.

## ABOUT THE AUTHOR

Craig Hedges is a father of four and husband of one. With his wife,
Tammy, they are raising a family of creative-minded kids through
interaction and conversation. Craig is the family storyteller, but is quickly
losing that status as his kids grow. There is never a deficit of imagination in
the Hedges house. Craig's love for stories, however, has led to this writing.
This should be the beginning of many more stories to come based on life
and the struggles we all endure.

Made in the USA
Columbia, SC
09 December 2017